WELSH CONVICT WOMEN

No, no—surely not! My God—
not more of those damned whores!
Never have I known worse women!

(*Lt. Clarke of the First Fleet on sighting
the Second Fleet coming into Sydney Harbour*)

WELSH CONVICT WOMEN

A study of women transported
from Wales to Australia, 1787-1852

by

Deirdre Beddoe

STEWART WILLIAMS PUBLISHERS
BARRY

First published September, 1979

© *Deirdre Beddoe*

ISBN 0 900807 33 4

Printed in Wales by
D. Brown and Sons Ltd., Cowbridge and Bridgend

To Katie

CONTENTS

PREFACE

This book is the result of my curiosity about the history of women in Wales. Normally it is very difficult to trace the lives of women in the past because their activities were so rarely recorded. Criminal women, however, are an exception. When they 'went wrong' and clashed with the law, their names were taken and recorded for posterity. When I came to dip into the records of court cases, and read the tales of crimes, I became interested in the sentences passed on these petty offenders. Sometimes women were sentenced to be stripped to the waist, paraded through the streets and whipped, sometimes they were set to hard labour for periods of months or years in local gaols and houses of correction, and sometimes they were sentenced 'to be transported to His Majesty's colonies beyond the Seas.' The last phrase—'beyond the Seas'—caught my imagination. At first it meant America, but it soon meant the long voyage to Australia and lifelong exile there. It is with the women who were sentenced to transportation by courts in Wales and who actually sailed on that very long journey to Australia that this book is concerned.

For me, tracking down the Welsh female transportees through records held in Wales, in London and in Australia has meant fascinating and exciting detective work. Many people have helped and encouraged me and I wish to thank them all.

I particularly wish to thank Jennifer Louise Homer, Luned Meredith, Eileen Hannaford and Muriel Bowen-Evans for a great deal of help and encouragement. My thanks also go to H.D. and I.C. and to my colleagues at the Polytechnic of Wales who have given me a wide variety of assistance. Many Librarians and Archivists have been tremendously helpful to me and I wish to thank them, especially Ms. McRae, Principal Archivist of the Archives Office of Tasmania, the Archivists and staff of the National Library of Wales, Aberystwyth; of Glamorgan County Record Office, of the Mitchell Library, Sydney, and the National Library of Australia, Canberra, and the Public Record Office, London.

I am also very grateful to the following bodies for permission to use illustrations: National Maritime Museum, London; National Library of

Australia, Canberra, for permission to publish from its own and from the Rex Nan Kivell Collection; Radio Times Hulton Picture Library, London; Australian Information Service, Australia House, London; National Library of Wales, Aberystwyth, and Tasmanian State Archive Office, Hobart, Tasmania.

My thanks also go to my publisher, Mr. Stewart Williams, whose efficiency has added to the pleasure of publishing.

DEIRDRE BEDDOE
February, 1979

Chapter 1

TRANSPORTATION: THE SYSTEM AND THE FEMALE CONVICTS

> For fourteen long years I am sentenced
> For fourteen long years and a day
> For meeting a bloke in the area
> And sneaking his ticker away.

Botany Bay

THE transportation of convicts, male and female, to far flung parts of the British Empire formed an integral part of the penal system in the eighteenth and nineteenth centuries. Transportation was the punishment for a wide variety of crimes—many of them petty. The theft of a small item—a handkerchief, an apron, a cheese, a single copper coin, a watch—could lead its perpetrator to life-long exile. Most of the women examined in this book stole just such items from houses or shops or gentlemen's pockets. Their punishment ranged from a *minimum* of seven years to a maximum of life to be spent in the penal colonies of Australia.

Transportation, as a punishment, had certain obvious advantages for the British government. It was expected to be cheap—far cheaper than keeping prisoners in gaols and bridewells at home, or building new-style penitentiaries. It had the further appeal of removing elements of the so called 'dangerous' classes from these shores. As George Bernard Shaw was later to observe, 'All social problems of all countries can be got rid of by extirpating the inhabitants.' The dread of exile was supposed to deter other potential malefactors from the paths of evil whilst those who actually were transported might be hoped, in some undefined way, to reform in a warmer climate. In fact, little thought was given to the convicts themselves. The main aim of transportation was punishment rather than the reformation of the offender. Jeremy Bentham, a reformer and opponent of transportation, seems to capture government thinking when he put the following words in the mouth of an imaginary judge. 'I sentence you, but to what I know not; perhaps to storm and shipwreck, perhaps to infectious disorders, perhaps to famine, perhaps to be massacred by savages, perhaps to be devoured by wild beasts. Away—take your chance; perish or prosper, suffer or enjoy; I rid myself of the sight of you.' Yet another advantage that the government at home could expect from the policy of penal transportation was the economic development of the colonies and hence Britain's enhancement as an imperial power.

The idea of punishment through exile was not a new one. Banishment was a punishment in operation in Britain since medieval times and transportation proper was established by an act of Parliament of 1717 (4. Geo I c.2). The act states:

> And whereas, in many of his Majesty's colonies and plantations in America, there is a great want of servants etc., be it enacted that any person convicted of any offence for which he is liable to be whipt or burnt on the hand or shall have been ordered to any workhouse . . . may be sent to some of his Majesty's colonies and plantations in America.

Following this act, transportation to America became a common punishment for certain felonies. It has been calculated that about 30,000 prisoners were conveyed from Britain to America during the eighteenth century. The outbreak of the American war of Independence in 1775 put an end to this practice. The government now sought alternative dumping grounds for its undesirables and a House of Commons committee reported that, 'transportation to unhealthy places, in place of sending better citizens, may be desirable.' West Africa was given serious consideration as a destination for transportees and certainly courts sentenced people there. Mary Watkins, a nineteen-year-old girl, from the parish of Saint Andrews, Glamorgan, was sentenced by the court of Quarter Sessions held at Cowbridge in April 1786 to be transported to the Coast of Africa for seven years. Her crime? Stealing clothes worth 6d. But Africa was not deemed suitable and other projects such as sending prisoners down coal mines or into the dangerous manufacture of lead were fleetingly considered. By the mid 1780s Australia, recently reached by Captain Cook, was being given serious attention as a possible penal colony. The scheme to develop Botany Bay, New South Wales, as a penal colony and so take the strain off the over-crowded gaols at home was announced in 1787. In the same year the First Fleet, carrying 586 male and 192 female convicts, sailed on its horrific voyage to Botany Bay.

For almost eighty years after the departure of the First Fleet, convicts were sent to the Australian penal colonies. The colonies were New South Wales, in Eastern Australia and Van Diemen's Land, now Tasmania, off the southern coast of the mainland. To these two colonies male and female convicts were sent. The year 1852 virtually marks the end of the transportation era but male convicts were sent to Western Australia between 1850 and 1868, at the request of that colony, which was suffering from an acute labour shortage.

12

The convict vessel *Morley* under way
National Maritime Museum, Greenwich

Between 1787 and 1852 no less than 147,580 convicts were transported to New South Wales and Van Diemen's Land. Of this total number, 24,960 were women. Of these women, nearly 300 came from the Welsh counties, including Monmouthshire. It is this group of 300 Welsh women with which this book is concerned.

How did the legal process work, which was to transform a dairy maid in Carmarthenshire or a laundress in Cardiff into a convict in New South Wales or Van Diemen's Land? The process was alarmingly simple. A young woman servant (and the transported females were young), might steal an item of clothing from her mistress—a petticoat, a hat, a gown. The mistress would report her to the police. The girl would be taken to the magistrate and formally charged at the instigation of her mistress. She would then be detained at the local prison awaiting trial. She would appear before one of the following courts, the court of Quarter Sessions (held each quarter in every county), the court of Great Sessions (held in Wales until its abolition in 1830) or, after 1830, in the Assize court. When tried and found guilty at one of these courts, the criminal would be sentenced to transportation for a set period, usually of seven years, fourteen years or life. Frequently delays occurred at this stage and some of the Welsh female transportees waited several years

before embarking for Australia. From the prison she would be transferred to the port of embarkation in southern England. The destination, to which she was to be conveyed, would be decided by the
Secretary of State. Upon completion of the long and arduous sea
voyage, it was provided that the convict was to be 'delivered to the
Governor of the Colony and that the Governor shall have property of
the service of the convict for the term of his transportation.'

Once the female convict arrived in Australia, the punishment she
received was of a very different nature from that she would have under-
gone in gaol in Britain. Basically, there were two elements to the punishment of females in Australia—confinement in one of the female
'factories' and assignment as a servant (some would say slave) to a
colonist. If she were industrious, virtuous and above all lucky, the
female convict would obtain a 'ticket of leave', or pardon, some years
before the official expiry of her sentence. But exile was for most female
convicts life long. The government issued no return tickets to convicts
and whereas male convicts had the chance of working a passage back to
Britain, women did not.

Before turning specifically to the Welsh women, it is important to
state two facts very clearly. Firstly, criminal women in general and convict women in particular have suffered from a universally bad press. So
consistently and effusively condemnatory is that press, that one has to
cut one's way through a mass of damning statements to begin to reach
the factual evidence.

Women were seen by eighteenth and nineteenth century contemporaries as falling within either one or the other of the two categories in
which the Judeo-Christian tradition has customarily relegated them, i.e.
the exclusively good or the exclusively bad. Criminal women were, of
course, *exclusively* bad. They were allowed no mitigating features. Only
a very small minority of their contemporaries, including Elizabeth Fry,
made any attempt to understand their condition. This rigid categorising
of women into the wholly good, like the Virgin Mary, or the wholly
bad, like Eve the Temptress, coloured much nineteenth-century thinking and writing on criminal women. An anonymous writer in the
Cornhill Magazine in 1866 well illustrates a nineteenth-century view of
criminal women.

> Again, it is notorious that a bad man—we mean one whose evil
> training had led him into crime—is not so vile as a bad woman. If
> we take a man and woman guilty of a similar offence in the eye of
> the law, we shall invariably find that there is more hope of in-
> fluencing the former than the latter. Equally criminal in one sense,
> in another sense there is a difference. The man's nature may be
> said to be hardened, the woman's destroyed. Women of this stamp

are generally so bold and unblushing in crime, so indifferent to right and wrong, so lost to all sense of shame, so destitute of the instincts of womanhood, that they may be more justly compared to wild beasts than to women. To say the least, the honour of womanhood requires that a new appellation be invented for them.

And again:

Criminal women, as a class, are found to be more uncivilised than the savage, more degraded than the slave, less true to all natural and womanly instincts than the untutored squaw of the North American Indian tribe. Let us look at their habits first—at their antecedents last: this was the order of the writer's experience. From the mass of evil habits that these women have accumulated, it is not easy to select illustrations that shall convey a vivid impression to the reader's mind. As a class they are guilty of lying, theft, unchastity, drunkenness, slovenliness. To finish the picture, it may be added, they are ignorant, so obtuse, that instruction might as well be given in an unknown tongue, so little do they understand it. Lying may be said to be their native language.

Jelinger C. Symons, in his work, *Tactics for the Times, as regards the Condition and Treatment of the Dangerous Classes*, was in little doubt about the evil character of some women.

So true is it that the extremes of vice as well as virtue co-exist in the female character. In the great revolution of France, and again, the last one, the most inhuman atrocities were perpetrated by women. Of the crime classes in England there can be little doubt that the criminal mind is quite as strong in women as in men. The lesser number of female offences arises, it is to be feared, chiefly from their lesser power rather than their better disposition. This view derives confirmation from the fact, that wherever women are much employed in masculine pursuits which tend to increase their power and opportunities of committing offences, the proportion of female to male offenders increases.

Similarly, the transportees have been almost universally condemned. Many contemporary writers denounced the female transportees *en masse* and regarded them as a sub species, an untouchable caste of near monsters. The following statements will serve to illustrate contemporary revulsion to the convict women. Lieutenant Colonel Henry Breton, appearing before the 1837 Commission of Inquiry into Transportation pulled no punches. On convict women he says, 'They are as bad as it is possible for human beings to be, the female convicts.' When asked if they were dissolute women, he replied, 'Shockingly so; they are

15

drunken, they are everything that is bad.' Thomas MacQueen, an Australian magistrate calls them, 'the most disgusting objects that ever graced the female form.' Again, as with the case of criminal women in general, the consensus of contemporary opinion was that the convict women were far worse than the men. W. B. Ullatorne asked, 'What shall I say of the female convict, acknowledged to be worse and far more difficult of reformation than the man? Her general character is immodesty, drunkeness and the most horrible language.' Yet again, one James Mudie stated, 'Of their character, I should say, in fact, that they are worse than the men in all descriptions of vice; you can have no conception of their depravity of character.'

It almost goes without saying that contemporaries regarded all convict women as prostitutes. To quote James Mudie again—'They all smoke and drink and in fact, to speak in plain language, I consider them all prostitutes.' They were, in Lieutenant Clarke's words, 'damned whores.' In short, the contemporary condemnations of the women are legion. We should not unquestioningly accept these criticisms and we must recognise the prejudices behind them. It must be one of the tasks of this book to try to find out the truth, at least as regards the Welsh group of transportees. The second fact, which needs to be stated with absolute clarity, concerns the reason why women were transported. Were women, like men, transported simply because they had committed crimes, or was there a more sinister reason behind the transportation of females?

There is ample evidence to confirm that the main reason women were transported was for the sexual gratification of both free and convict males. There was a great disparity between the male and female populations in the penal colonies. If one looks at the convict population of New South Wales, set out below, the great disparity between the sexes is clear.

Convict Population of New South Wales

Year	Males	Females	Total
1788	529	188	717
1790	297	70	367
1800	1,230	328	1,558
1805	1,561	516	2,077
1819	8,920	1,066	9,986
1828	16,442	1,544	17,986
1836	25,254	2,577	27,831
1841	23,844	3,133	26,977
Total	78,077	9,422	87,499

M. Weidenhofer, *The Convict Years*

Again, if one includes the free emigrants (but excludes the military), the overwhelming preponderance of males is striking. D. D. Heath, an expert on demography, presented the following evidence to the Select Committee on Transportation in 1837.

Besides these results of the moral condition of the convicts whom we send to people these countries, there are other, and perhaps worse consequences, arising from the great disproportion between male and female criminals. The extent of this evil will be at once manifest from a statement of the population returns. According to the census of 1833, there were in New South Wales, exclusive of the military.

			Free
Above 12 years old	Males	...	17,542
	Females	...	8,521
Under 12 years old	Males	...	5,256
	Females	...	4,931

Convict

Males	...	...	...	...	21,846
Females ...	...	...	...	...	2,698

TOTAL:	Males ...	44,644
	Females ...	16,150

In Van Diemen's Land no distinction is made in the age; it appears however, that excluding military, there were, in 1834,

Free		*Convict*		
Males	... 12,525	Males	...	13,664
Females	... 8,561	Females	...	1,874

TOTAL:	Males ...	26,240
	Females ...	10,496

From this it appears that Van Diemen's Land is in a little better state than New South Wales, though, from the defect above noticed, we cannot exactly estimate the real difference. It must be observed, that the state of things indicated by these tables cannot be considered as tending of themselves soon to pass away, though undoubtedly, if transportation were abolished, and the free emigration of families encouraged, the effects would soon be sensible.

17

Female Emigration

TO

AUSTRALIA.

COMMITTEE:

EDWARD FORSTER, Esq. Chairman.
SAMUEL HOARE, Esq.
JOHN TAYLOR, Esq.
THOMAS LEWIN, Esq.
S. H. STERRY, Esq.

CHARLES HOLTE BRACEBRIDGE, Esq.
JOHN S. REYNOLDS, Esq.
JOHN PIRIE, Esq.
CAPEL CURE, Esq.
WILLIAM CRAWFORD. Esq.

CHARLES LUSHINGTON, Esq.
JOHN ABEL SMITH, Esq. M.P.
GEORGE LONG, Esq.
COLONEL PHIPPS,
NADIR BAXTER, Esq.
CAPTAIN DANIEL PRING, R.N

The Committee for promoting the Emigration

OF

Single Women

To AUSTRALIA, acting under the Sanction of His Majesty's Secretary of State for the Colonies, HEREBY GIVE NOTICE, That

THE SPLENDID TEAK-BUILT SHIP

"David Scott," of 773 Tons Register,

GRAVESEND

on Thursday 10th of July next,

(Beyond which day she will on no account be detained) direct for

SYDNEY.

On payment of FIVE POUNDS only.

Single Women and Widows of good Character, from 15 to 30 Years of Age, desirous of bettering their Condition by Emigrating to that healthy and highly prosperous Colony, where the number of Females compared with the entire Population is greatly deficient, and where consequently from the great demand for Servants, and other Female Employments, the Wages are comparatively high, may obtain a Passage

Those who are unable to raise even that Sum here, may, when approved by the Committee, go *without any Money Payment whatever*, as their Notes of Hand will be taken, payable in the Colony within a reasonable time after their arrival, when they have acquired the means to do so: in both cases the Parties will have the advantage of the **Government Grant** in aid of their Passage.

The Females who proceed by this Conveyance will be taken care of on their first Landing at Sydney. They will find there a List of the various Situations to be obtained, and of the Wages offered, and will be perfectly free to make their own Election; they will not be bound to any person, or subjected to any restraint, but will be, to all intentsand purposes, perfectly free to act and decide for themselves.

Females in the Country who may desire to avail themselves of the important advantages thus offered them, should apply by Letter to "The Emigration Committee, London," under Cover addressed to "The UNDER SECRETARY of STATE, COLONIAL DEPARTMENT, LONDON." It will be necessary that the Application be accompanied by a Certificate of Character from the Resident Minister of the Parish, or from some other respectable persons to whom the Applicant may be known; but the Certificate of the Resident Minister is in all cases most desirable. Such Females as may find it expedient may, when approved by the Committee as fit persons to go by this Conveyance, be boarded temporarily in London, prior to Embarkation, on Payment of 7s. per Week.

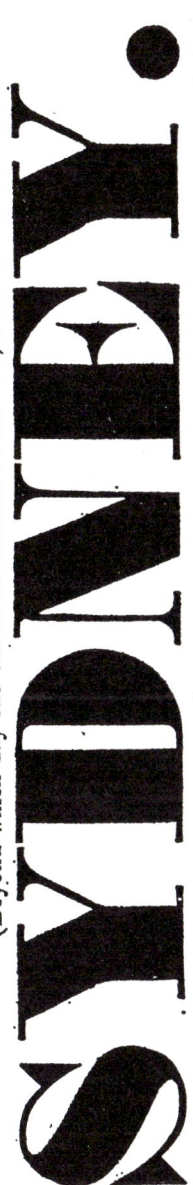 All Applications made under cover in the foregoing manner, or personally, will receive early Answers, and all necessary Information, by applying to

JOHN MARSHALL, Agent to the Committee, 26, Birchin Lane, Cornhill, London.

EDWARD FORSTER, *Chairman.*

LONDON, 1st May, 1834.

NOTE.—The Committee have the satisfaction to state that of 217 Females who went out by the "Bussorah Merchant," 180 obtained good Situations within three Days of their Landing, and the remainder were all well placed within a few Days, under the advice of a Ladies' Committee, formed in the Colony expressly to aid the Females on their arrival.

By Authority:

PRINTED BY JOSEPH HARTNELL, FLEET STREET, FOR HIS MAJESTY'S STATIONERY OFFICE.

Posters encouraging single women to emigrate showed concern over the shortage of women in Australia

H. M. Stationery Office, 1834

Heath observed that if transportation was not abolished and that 'if the colony were left entirely to itself, very many years must elapse before this evil would right itself.' In fact, Heath thought at least a hundred years would need to elapse before there was any approximation to equality of numbers between the sexes in Australia.

The British government was greatly concerned to rectify the imbalance in the sexes in the colonies and consequently, it would seem, that harsher sentences were imposed on women than men. 'Whereas only the more hardened male offenders under sentence of transportation were actually transported to the colonies, all women under sentence, provided that they were healthy and under forty-five were transported.' This was government policy! So desperately anxious was the British government to supply the colonies with women that in 1787 Governor Philip received the following order:—

> And whereas, as from the great disproportion of female convicts to those of the males who are put under your superintendance, it appears advisable that a further number of the latter should be introduced into the new intended settlement, you are, whenever the *Sirius* or the tender shall touch at any of the islands in those seas, to instruct their commanders to take aboard any of the women who may be disposed to accompany them to the said settlement.

D. D. Heath, whose observations on the Australian population are mentioned above, debated whether or not women should be transported. He saw little hope of any punishment, at home or abroad, reforming the female transportees and thought the decision on whether or not to transport them should depend entirely on whether or not the colonies needed the female numbers. 'The resolution of the question', he wrote, 'mainly depends on whether the injury or benefit of their presence in the colonies, *in their present state of population, will preponderate.*'

In other words, the decision whether to transport individual women, including first offenders, depended on the colonial balance of population. It had nothing to do with the reformation of offenders. In short, a woman, found guilty by a court of an offence, was more likely to find herself actually sailing to Botany Bay or Van Diemen's Land than her male counterpart. When she reached Australia the role expected of her was clear and consequently her chance of reformation minimal. These two facts—the universal condemnation of the convict women by contemporaries and the knowledge of the government's ulterior motive in sending them to Australia—will throw light on a study of the Welsh convict women.

20

Turning to the Welsh convict women themselves, fortunately they have left many traces in the records. It is possible to state who actually sailed and to discover a good deal of detail about them, including their native place, occupation, appearance and character. In many instances fairly full records survive telling the tale of the crimes which led to the women being transported. On the voyage itself, diaries, ships logs and convict records enable one to reconstruct the conditions on board ship for the women and for the children whom they took with them. Finally, when the women arrived in Australia, their activities and conduct were kept under careful surveillance and noted down, so that we can still catch glimpses of the lives of the exiled Welsh women in the colonies.

Chapter 2

ORIGINS, APPEARANCES AND OCCUPATIONS

My true love she was beautiful
My true love she was young
Her eyes were like two diamonds bright
And silvery was her tongue
And silvery was her tongue my boys
Although she's far away
She's taken a trip on a government ship
Ten thousand miles away.

Ten Thousand Miles Away

WE know exactly who the Welsh convict women were. The British Government, acting in its capacity as gaoler, was most careful to note the names of all those in its care. As the convicts were herded aboard the ships at the dockside, a full register of their names was taken. These records survive in full. They are organised under the name of the ship and listed underneath is the name, county and date of trial of each woman. There are 18 volumes of such registers, containing the names of Welsh women, kept among the *Home Office, Convict Collection* in the Public Record Office, London.

The following table shows the number of women, who were sentenced to transportation and who actually sailed from each Welsh county:

Anglesey	6
Breconshire	20
Caernarvonshire	16
Cardiganshire	1
Carmarthenshire	22
Denbighshire	28
Flintshire	5
Glamorgan	71
Merionethshire	6
Monmouthshire	60
Montgomeryshire	22
Pembrokeshire	17
Radnorshire	9
Total:	283

The name of each Welsh transportee is listed under county headings in the appendices.

Quite obviously the amount of crime committed in any county will be linked to the size of the population of that county and the two densely populated Welsh counties of Glamorgan and Monmouthshire stand out in the table of transportees. But not only were these two counties the most highly populated in Wales, they were also the most industrialised and consequently the most urbanised of the Welsh counties. It will be useful to pause briefly to look at the background of crime in the industrialised areas of South Wales to see the conditions which were to produce so many of the Welsh convict women.

The transportation era coincided with the Industrial Revolution in Wales. The development of the iron industry, centering on Merthyr, and the mining of coal in the Rhondda valleys began dramatically to transform South Wales. From being a largely rural area, where most of the inhabitants lived in villages, it became an industrialised region with boom towns. Merthyr's growth was spectacular. A mere hamlet in 1750, Merthyr became the largest town in Wales in 1801 with a population of 7,700. In 1851 it still maintained its leading position with a population of over 35,000. The population of Cardiff too rose very rapidly and its growth has been compared to that of Chicago! Profiting first from the development of iron and then, even more so, from coal, in its hinterland, Cardiff rose to the ranks of a leading port. In the fifty years from 1801 to 1851 Cardiff's population increased at least ninefold, from under 2,000 in 1801 to over 18,000 in 1851. By 1861 it had reached 33,000. Copper, coal and shipping were the main springs of Swansea's development and, although ousted by Merthyr in 1801 as Wales' largest town, Swansea also experienced considerable growth.

The rapid development of industries and the mushroom growth of towns produced great problems and stresses. Overcrowded housing, inadequate sanitation, disease, a high death rate, crime and prostitution were key features of life in the South Wales towns. Cardiff with its phenomenal growth rate provides a good example of the problems stemming from rapid expansion. Its death rate was high—30 per 1,000 between 1842 and 1848. Typhus struck frequently and there were major outbreaks of cholera. Working class families, especially the Irish, lived in abject squalor with up to twenty inhabitants to a room in Stanley Street. That figure *excludes* casual lodgers who were staying the odd few nights! Five hundred people lived in the twenty-seven two-roomed houses in Landore Court. A few privies were shared by whole courts. The docks area of Butetown, with its shifting population of sailors, was already the scene of knife fights and brawls and was foreshadowing its fierce reputation of the second half of the nineteenth century. Crime and prostitution were on the increase.

Landore Court (at rear of St Mary Street), Cardiff, in 1891
Cardiff Central Library

The rise in crime was, in fact, a national phenomenon. Between 1805 and 1850 the number of committals per 100,000 of the population trebled. This increase in crime was truly spectacular. Conditions in some counties were real breeding grounds of criminality. Parts of Monmouthshire and Breconshire, notably the iron districts, were just such places. Jellinger C. Symons, who knew Welsh conditions well and who had acted as a commissioner in the infamous inquiry into the state of Education in Wales of 1846-7, had the following to say:

> The iron districts are not only more criminal than others (except the metropolis), but they possess features of moral debasement and abandonment peculiar to themselves. There is no class of industry in which the welfare of the labourers is more grossly neglected by the employers. This community has risen chiefly by immigration from most parts of Wales and England. Whatever is unsettled or lawless, or roving or characterless among working men, as long as bodily strength subsists, has felt an attraction to this district and a surety of ready acceptance and good wages, which very few other districts have afforded in so great a degree . . .

Symons had a special word to say about Welsh criminal women. In the iron areas, he states, there was a higher proportion of criminal women than in any other type of industrialised region, such as the mining or cotton areas.

> As we have before seen, the lawless vices and rude habits of the men are communicated to the women. In murderous offences by females, no other district (not excepting London) affords so many instances. Even in offences against property committed with violence, the women there more largely participate than elsewhere. This is in some degree owing to the masculine pursuits in the works and at the pits, which degrade them to the habits and brutalities of the men.

In fact, Monmouthshire in the years 1846-7 had the greatest increase in crime of any English county including Middlesex in which London was incorporated! But not only were the working classes a threat to property, they were also a moral danger. Emanating upwards from the lower orders were the vices of prostitution and drink.

Prostitution was a normal part of life in the growing new towns, which had almost a frontier air. The Rev. Henry Richards, writing in 1866, sought to project a shining image of a virtuous, respectable and non-conformist Wales. But the amount of prostitution in the principality was rather an obstacle to his aims. The only way he could overcome this, was by excluding Glamorgan altogether and saying it was not truly Welsh. Its inclusion would certainly have ruined his whole argument.

Suffice it here to say that in Cardiff alone in the 1860s, it was alleged, there were 120 brothels and 420 known prostitutes (and that was within the city boundaries, which excluded Canton and Roath). The saloons and dance halls of Butetown were their haunts and the sailors, and a sprinkling of the disapproving middle classes, their clientele.

The incidence of drunkenness, like crime, rose during the industrialisation of South Wales. The public house was certainly a more enjoyable place to spend an evening than a crowded slum lodging house, and drink afforded, relatively cheaply, oblivion from the wretchedness of daily life. There are quite close links between drink and crime, which are discussed later. Some of the transportees were 'drinkers' and certainly some of the victims of robberies were incapacitated through drink.

But although a few counties provide a high proportion of the Welsh convict women they do not account for them all. About half of the women came from the other Welsh counties, from quiet country areas and small hamlets where life was as yet hardly touched by the Leviathan of industrialisation. These girls and women were employed on farms, out of doors or indoors. Some were married to farm labourers, some worked as servant girls in remote country houses and others in small market towns. Really, we ought to see the Welsh convict women as a mixture, with some coming from the old style rural Wales and others from the new industrial Wales.

As for the language which they spoke, undoubtedly many were Welsh speaking. But the records only mention that they could speak Welsh if they could not speak English. At the court case of one young Carmarthenshire woman an interpreter had to be employed because the woman knew no English at all. Imagine having the sentence of transportation passed on one when one could not understand the proceedings. Some women from North Wales knew no English at all. Some of these came from Anglesey and Caernarvonshire. That does not seem surprising to us nowadays. But somehow it takes one back with a jolt to read of Elizabeth James, a native of Cardiff, who was transported in the 1840s, as being able only to speak English very badly. It is interesting too that these exclusively Welsh speakers could also read and write in Welsh. However, in writing of the origins of the Welsh women transportees, it is necessary to be careful. Not all the women *tried* in a county were natives of that county. In fact the evidence suggests quite a bit of movement by young women around the country . . . looking for jobs, seasonal or for longer, looking for husbands or maybe just good times. We are used to reading of the influx of men into areas where new industries were being developed but no study has been made of women's mobility. If we look at the women transported from Glamorgan, we find that many were natives but that there were also young women from rural Pembrokeshire, Breconshire, Herefordshire and also Monmouthshire. Even the native Glamorgan girls came often from tiny villages into the big job and crime centres of Cardiff or Swansea. Movement into Monmouthshire of criminal women is quite striking. They came from Herefordshire, Cardiganshire, Hampshire, Bristol and Gloucestershire. A handful came from Ireland . . . but they were only a few so it will not do to blame all crime on the Irish. A few came into Monmouthshire from Scotland, for example, from Glasgow and Ayr. Among Carmarthenshire's twenty-two female transportees was a woman from Cornwall, one from London and another from Stoke-on-Trent. Finally, even in the very rural counties of Wales some of the transportees came from distant places. A Galway woman was transported from Flintshire and a Scottish woman from Anglesey. There really was more movement of young women than has generally been thought.

As regards the physical appearance of the convict women, we are fortunate in possessing full descriptions. There was a clear need for very detailed descriptions of each convict. In case they should escape a 'Wanted Notice' could draw on the meticulous information at hand. The Australian authorities were most painstaking in their regard for detail.

The following are typical:

Wheeler, Eliza	*Garland Grove*
Trade	Dairy Maid
Height (without shoes)	4' 11¾"
Age	20 years
Complexion	Fair
Head	Round
Hair	Dark Brown
Whiskers	—
Visage	Round
Forehead	Medium Height
Eyebrows	Dark Brown
Eyes	Light Blue
Nose	Medium
Mouth	Small
Chin	Round
Native Place	Herefordshire
Remarks	Small cut on left thumb. Brown mole on left cheek. Black mark on front tooth.

Watkins, Eleanor   *Cadet*

Trade	Dairy woman
Height (without shoes)	5' 3½"
Age	23
Complexion	Fresh
Head	Round
Hair	Dark Brown
Whiskers	—
Visage	Broad
Forehead	Medium
Eyebrows	Dark Brown
Eyes	Blue
Nose	Short, thick
Mouth	Medium
Chin	Dimpled
Native Place	Brecon
Remarks	Freckled, J.M.G.R. on left arm; scar on third finger of right hand.

Williams, Margaret   *Tory*

Trade	House-maid
Height (without shoes)	4' 9½"
Age	35
Complexion	Dark
Head	Round
Hair	Black
Whiskers	—
Visage	Small
Forehead	Medium
Eyebrows	Dark Brown
Eyes	Hazel
Nose	Small
Mouth	Small
Chin	Small
Native Place	Cardiff
Remarks	Front teeth prominent. Scar under right eye. W.B. upper right arm.

Watkins Eleanor

Transported for Stealing from the person Gaol report

Tried Glamorgan 4 April 1848 Grand Second Conviction Single States her offence stealing

Embarked Surrey from David Gaol at Glamorgan 18 months

Arrived 14 April 1849 P R 18 months in the town

Trade.	Height.	Age.	Complex.	Head.	Hair.	Whiskers.	Visage.	Forehead.	Eyebrows.	Eyes.	Nose	Mouth.	Chin.	Native Place.
Dairy Woman	5 3¾	20	Fresh	Round	dark brown	—	Round Medium	Medium	dark brown	blue	short thick	Medium	Dimpled	Brecon South Wales

Marks Freckled J. M. E. R. on left arm scar on third finger of right hand

Period of Gang Probation

Station of Gang

Class 3 1st 10/9/49

Offences & Sentences.

T.L. 18/11/51
J.C.
Conditional Pardon Apd 24/1/53

Remarks.

Eleanor Watkins' criminal record and description
State Library of Tasmania

NAME, *Jenkin Ann.* **No.** *111*

Trade
Height without shoes
Age
Complexion
Head
Hair
Whiskers
Visage
Forehead
Eyebrows
Eyes
Nose
Mouth
Chin
Remarks

Description of Ann Jenkins, convict
State Library of Tasmania

Edwards, Margaret	*The Edward*
Trade	Household servant
Height (without shoes)	4′ 11″
Age	19
Complexion	Dark
Head	Small
Hair	Black
Visage	Small
Forehead	High
Eyebrows	Dark Brown
Eyes	Dark Brown
Nose	M.L. (i.e. medium length)
Mouth	Large
Chin	Medium

Native Place   Swansea

Remarks   M.E. on right arm. Brown
                             mole left side of chin. Deep
                             scar corner right eye.

Dark hair and eyes predominate among the Welsh women. The shape of face, nose, eyebrows and chin were all carefully noted and such features as dimples, turned up noses or double chins were faithfully recorded. Complexions were also entered into the records and many of the girls and women were described as ruddy or fresh: these healthy complexions, not surprisingly, frequently apply to the farm girls. Yet others were dark or sallow. Any distinguishing mark was particularly interesting to the authorities as a means of identification. Such special 'marks' included freckles. Other women were described as 'pockpitted' —a sharp reminder of the prevalence of such serious and disfiguring diseases. Scars and moles were always recorded. One woman is described as having:

> Mole on right cheek and three on face, scar on right arm and a scar on left thumb, scar on left side of forehead.

Actually, moles were regarded by some criminologists as a mark of dreadful degeneracy! Even the loss of a nail is noted in one woman, another was 'blind in the left eye and pockpitted', and yet another had 'lost some of front teeth upper jaw' and was lame. Sometimes the women are recorded as wearing a ring—a surprising piece of official tolerance, especially since not all the ring wearers were married.

Finally one of the most striking distinguishing marks were tattoos. Many of the convict women were tattooed. They were often city girls and very often prostitutes. A few women, transported from other parts of Britain, had been tattooed with poignant sentiments such as:

> Alfred Whitfield I love to the heart
>   or
> William Jessie when this you see
> Remember me and bear me in your mind
> Let all the world say what they will
> Speak of me as you find

None of the Welsh women were inscribed with such eloquent sentiments. But Ann Lee, tried at Monmouth, had the following tattooed on her upper right arm—the initials F.S.J.C.B. and a heart. On her left arm was M.M. together with a design of a Jug, a Glass and the word HOPE. Ann Evans of Pembrokeshire had her lower left arm tattooed with the name Beynon Richards and the symbol of a heart. On her right arm were her own initials and those of J.E. Perhaps J.E. had replaced

31

Beynon in Ann's affections. Actually many of the tattoos were simply initials. Elizabeth Griffiths of Swansea must hold some sort of record. Her right arm read C.W.E.W.R.A.M.M.E.G.M.M.D.E. and her left, J.R.D.G.J.G.M.C.W.C.

During the nineteenth century a very serious study was undertaken of 'criminal types'. It aimed at proving the existence of a set of physical characteristics common to many criminals. It all seems rather ludicrous now and dreadfully prejudiced but people such as Caesar Lombroso, a leading Italian anthropologist, undertook this work with great solemnity. He measured skulls, weighed the brains (of those already hanged), examined the noses, earlobes, foreheads, eyes, jaws, legs and feet of the convicted criminals and prostitutes. His conclusions include:

> Female thieves, and above all prostitutes, are inferior to moral women in cranial capacity and circumference, and their cranial diameters are less; but, on the other hand, their facial diameters are larger, especially in the jaw. Criminals have the darker hair and eyes, and this holds good also to a certain extent of prostitutes, in whom fair and red hair now surpasses and now approximates to the normal.

Lombroso and his associates looked in great detail at the faces of criminal women and decided that receding foreheads, asymetrical faces and projecting cheek bones were all far more common in criminals than in normals. He thought criminal women often had a masculine look and a 'hard, cruel look to their faces'. On tattoos Lombroso wrote that this practice 'is so rare as to be practically non-existent'. Maybe that was true for the European criminals whom Lombroso examined in the later nineteenth century but it does not hold good for Welsh convict women in the first half of the century. Tattoos were very common among them. Lombroso adds an interesting sidelight. Parisian women's tattoos include the initials of both female and male lovers. I simply do not know the sex of the dear ones engraved on the Welsh women's arms. They may not all have been lovers. Ms. McRae, the Tasmanian archivist, has suggested to me that they could be other members of gangs. With some certainty one can link tattoos with prostitutes. I have never come across a 'clean living farm girl' bearing tattoos and it simply never was a genteel practice. No lady who swooned in a drawing room was ever hauled up by tattooed arms!

Contemporary observers in Wales usually stress the physical strength of working class women. Two such observers, both outsiders, and therefore seeing with fresh eyes, were Wirt Sykes and A. J. Munby. Wirt Sykes, American consul in Cardiff in the last century, was a keen observer of Welsh womanhood. He delighted in describing women of all kinds and the impression one gets from Sykes is of a hefty, physically strong breed of working women. He wrote of Carmarthenshire's 'giantesses' and, although he notes that their stature was unusual in Wales, he exulted in the power and strength of women in all parts of Wales. He was impressed by the women of the coal areas of the hinterland of South Wales and those down at the docks. Of the former, he wrote 'The Welsh woman of the collier class is a formidable antagonist', and, in describing the latter, he calls them 'sturdy charmers'.

A. J. Munby was another nineteenth-century visitor to Wales. Munby spent a great deal of his life looking at, drawing and taking photographs of working class girls. He mainly operated in the North of England but in the 1860s he came to Wales. He noted that his tour to South Wales was 'introducing me to grand hills and vallies of the mineral country and the splendid chaos of the iron works, and above all, the picturesque ways and frank and modest charms of the robust and fearless girls who work at these mountain mines.'

Clearly Welsh working class women were not the feeble and delicate dolls that Victorian middle class women came to be. The working women did extremely heavy work both in outside employment and in the home. Given the strength expected of women, it comes as something of a surprise to see from the convict records how very small many of them were. The shortest I have found was only 4' 8" tall and very many were under 5 feet. This is, I think, linked to national characteristics but also to poor diet and living standards.

A further piece of information which helps us to visualise the convict women is their ages. As one would expect, given the motive of the British government in providing women as objects of sexual gratification for the male population of Australia, the women were mainly young. Many were in their teens and many in their early twenties. A few examples of actual women will serve better here than pages of statistics.

Fanny Bennet of Montgomeryshire was aged 13 when she committed the crime which led to her transportation.

Ann Thomas of Glamorgan was 17 when she stole a wine glass.

Elizabeth Lewis of Monmouth was 18 when she took a piece of bacon.

Sarah Rees of Haverfordwest was 20 when she stole a gown.

Elizabeth Hughson of Brecon was 22 when she was transported for housebreaking.

Many others were in their twenties, a few in their thirties and only very few were older than that. Among the older women (and women in their forties were considered quite old ladies) were the following:

Catherine Lewis, aged 42, was tried at Brecon for stealing wood.

Mary Burns, aged 47, was tried in Pembrokeshire for stealing poultry.

Mary Williams, a farm servant of 61 was transported from Carmarthenshire for stealing clothing (although described as swarthy and wrinkled, her hair was still dark brown).

Mary Williams aged 65 from Kildare, was tried in Caernarvonshire for passing counterfeit coins.

As to the marital status of the convict women, the majority were single. Of 100 women transported from Wales to Van Diemen's Land, whose lives I have examined in detail, 60 said they were single. A further 17 said they were widows. Clearly only a minority were married. Of course, one problem is whether the women were telling the truth. The evidence for marital status usually comes from their own statements. The widows, in particular, may simply have said they were widows in order to form a new attachment and marry in Australia. Elizabeth Morgan, the mother of three children, said that her husband had died three months after her last confinement. Ann Pike said she was not certain if her husband was dead but that he had left her four years ago. Eliza Wheeler, whose description is given in full elsewhere, stated in gaol, 'I never said I was married . . . no one ever came to see me.' Who knows the truth in these cases? The story of Ann Jones, transported from Radnorshire, rings true to me. She had married a man called William Bannows and they had lived together for seven years. But one day Bannow's first wife turned up and seems to have been taken back by Bannows. Ann had to leave. But some women clearly lied. Ann Smith, the Irish woman already mentioned as being the great old age of 65 at the time of transportation, said that she had been tried with her husband but that he was now dead. But, on arrival in Australia, her husband, John Smith, a convict on the vessel *Pestonjee Bomanjee*, claimed that Mary was his wife! In fact, so keen were some women to be listed as widows that they arranged that letters should be posted from home, informing them of the sad deaths of their husbands.

Several of the women, single or married, cohabited in regular and frequently long-lasting associations with men. There are a few statements from them such as that made by a single woman—'Father of my child, Charles Phillips with whom I lived three years', or from a

The convict ship *Mount Stuart Elphinstone*
National Maritime Museum, Greenwich

woman married to a soldier of the 45th Regiment—'Father of my child, Michael Nealan, I lived with him 15 months.'

Many convict women were mothers, though marital status had little bearing on this. Some had very large families. For example, Mary Lewis, a Carmarthenshire widow, had fourteen children and Charlotte Williams, from the same county had nine (three of whom were transported with her). Some other women had up to seven children but many had only one or two. This is explained by the extreme youth of many of the women. Many, of course, had more children in Australia. Women with young children, but not at the breast, took them with them to Australia. Several had up to three children on board and the story of these children will be told in Chapter 6.

Finally, what jobs did the convict women do? Many of them gave their employment as some form of domestic service. Most commonly they were housemaids, kitchen maids or simply servants. A few said they were cooks or plain cooks. Others were laundresses—one of the most unpleasant and heaviest of all jobs. In Wales a high proportion gave their occupation as farm servants, dairy women, country servants or servants in husbandry. The latter two types of work seem to have been mainly outdoor work and women did at this period engage in a lot

35

of work on the land. Even the farm servants did some outdoor work, when required, as well as domestic duties in the farm house. When Ann Williams, a Welsh monoglot, aged 19 from Anglesey was asked her job she said, 'Farm servant, milk and wash.' Her answer puts one in mind of the sort of statement a young girl would have made at the country hiring fairs where men and women sought work.

The jobs of cook and dairy woman (which included the making of butter and cream) were skilled jobs. There were a few other occupations, given by the convict women, which would be designated as skilled. There were needlewomen, dressmakers, a shoe-binder, and a few nurses. One woman said she was a nursery governess and a needlewoman. She had no previous offences and her crime was rather out of the ordinary; she stole a letter containing £100. This suggests she was of a higher social class and from a different background to most convict women.

But although we can discover many details about the physical appearance, age, occupation and marital status of the women, one vital aspect demands attention. The tantalising question must be—What sort of women were they? It is to their characters and temperaments we must next turn.

Chapter 3

CHARACTER AND TEMPERAMENT

Oh, Maggie, Maggie May, they have taken you away
To slave upon that cold Van Diemen's shore!
For you robbed so many sailors and dosed so many whalers,
You'll never cruise down Lime Street anymore!

Maggie May

THERE we have it! In the words of Maggie May the popular image of all
female transportees is encapsulated. The convict woman was a wicked,
if captivating, whore, who robbed innocent men of their hard earned
wages. But this stereotyped convict-whore figure needs close scrutiny. If
one only looked at Australian evidence this picture would seem to be
one hundred per cent accurate, for the number of Australian statements
saying that all convict women were prostitutes is legion and cannot
seriously be doubted. But this does not mean to say that all English,
Irish, Scottish or Welsh women were prostitutes *in Britain*. In fact, it
seems quite clear that the convict system turned women into prostitutes.
They may not have been driven to this way of life in Britain but they
certainly were in Australia. At the most basic level of explanation of
their behaviour—with no beds provided for them by the authorities in
Australia, they prostituted themselves in order to obtain a bed and
shelter. If the crown was the font of justice in Britain then it was also
the royal pimp, responsible, either wittingly, or through neglect, for
wholesale prostitution in the penal colonies. It is a strange, but accurate, role in which to cast Queen Victoria.

Turning to the evidence as to whether or not the women were street
walkers in Britain, there are some startling revelations. H.S. Payne in
an analysis of 150 British female convicts sent to Tasmania between
1843-1853 shows that only 24% were designated prostitutes. In a similar
analysis which I have made of 100 Welsh women sent to Tasmania my
conclusions are not quite as favourable. My findings were that 50% of
the Welsh women convicts sent to Tasmania were designated prostitutes. It would seem that the Welsh women more readily turned to
this expedient or perhaps, more likely, their need was greater. Within
the group of Welsh prostitutes the high proportion of women from
Glamorgan is very striking and, of course, large scale prostitution is an

urban phenomenon. Yet even more rural Pembrokeshire could boast, or be reticent about, 45 houses of 'ill fame' listed in a government publication of the 1860s. But the important point is that about half of the Welsh female transportees were *not* prostitutes at all in Wales. It would be simply untrue to think of all girls and women transported as dissolute harlots and depraved fallen women, to use the parlance of the times. At least half the convict women may have been no more immoral than the rest of Welsh womanhood left behind in Wales.

As to the Welsh women who were whores it is easy to be morally censorious of them. But many of the women were driven to this lifestyle through sheer material need. Both Henry Mayhew and William Acton, who investigated prostitution and interviewed many women in the nineteenth century, concluded that poverty was the chief factor in turning women into prostitutes. Moreover, a dual standard is almost invariably applied when moral judgements are passed upon these women and upon the gentlemen who patronised them. The client creates a demand: the prostitute meets it. The woman is condemned and the client exonerated!

The visual image which comes to mind of the Welsh convict whore as a heavily painted, gaudily bedizened, creature of the night to be found on street corners and in public houses, is quite an accurate picture of some of them. This is likely to be the correct image for many of the tattooed street walkers of the port area of Cardiff. But other women were far from obviously prostitutes and only used this device as a means of supplementing their inadequate earnings. Most of these women were also house and kitchen maids and their prostitution was of this casual, supplementary nature. The occasional prostitute was not uncommon among working class women especially when times were very hard. Whereas men in bad years turned directly to crime, women, I suspect, turned to prostitution first and only then to crime. The temptation to earn more in one night than in two weeks at a sweated trade (if such a job was even available) is quite obvious. Nor should we have too nice or too sensitive a vision of working class morality. Propriety and 'decency' becomes alien to people who live fifteen or twenty to a room.

The experience of prostitution was hardly an ennobling one and the young dollymop (young working girl who has begun to practise as a prostitute) soon turned into the experienced and ravaged whore. The records speak of many of the women in Cardiff as having been 'on the town' 7 or 10 years. Remarks about some of the women made by their gaolers show the depths to which they had sunk. They are variously described as:

'a bad prostitute'
'a depraved prostitute'

38

'one of the very worst class of prostitutes'
or
'a common prostitute of the lowest grade'

Perhaps some of the saddest young women are those just setting out on the road to prostitution and who described themselves as having been 'on the town' for just two or three months.

Another important aspect concerning the character of the Welsh convict women is their degree of criminality. It is important to establish whether they were hardened old offenders or simply first (or even second) offenders. Again there is evidence from an all-British source to throw some light on the question. In Payne's statistical survey of British female convicts in Tasmania 1843-1853, 28% were first offenders and a further 37% had only one previous offence. In short c. 65% of this all-British sample were not professional and habitual criminals. Turning to the Welsh evidence based upon my survey of Welsh women in Tasmania the results are even more amazing:

35% had no previous convictions
43% had one previous conviction, in addition to the one for which they were being transported
and only
20% had more committals and may be regarded as regular criminals.

In short just about a third of all the Welsh women were first offenders and only about one fifth were old-timers at crime. This is an amazing illustration of the severity of the criminal law in action. What is also interesting is that a first time offender in Wales was more likely to be transported than a similar person in England.

It was quite possible for a woman to have committed a single petty offence, to be caught, sentenced and transported. A few examples will illustrate just how this could happen. Among first offenders was Ann Roberts, a 21-year-old farm servant, who appeared at Montgomery Assizes for stealing one cotton dress. Ann was described as a sober and industrious girl but nevertheless, upon being found guilty, she was transported for seven years. Another woman whose first conviction was punished by transportation was Margaret Insell. At 35 she was a widow with a child to support and with no particular skills to earn much money. She was described as a quiet woman and she did not turn to prostitution to supplement her earnings. She worked variously as a housemaid and a laundress. But she stole £2 from a man and for this first offence she too was transported for seven years. Invariably the first offenders only indulged in very small scale theft of such items as worn clothing or food or small sums of money. Just two more cases will demonstrate the pettiness of their crimes. Ann Watkins, a fair 19-year-old shoebinder from Monmouthshire, was convicted for the first time for stealing a piece of bacon and a loaf of bread. She was transported for ten years. Finally, Ellen Davies, a freckled 19-year-old 'nurse girl' from Brecon, working in Anglesey, was convicted of the first offence of burglary. This sounds serious but when one looks at what she stole its seriousness diminishes: she took a piece of cheese and a few rashers of bacon and for this in 1850, she received a seven year sentence of transportation. The offences may often have been petty, but the punishments were usually vicious.

Of those women twice convicted, their two offences were usually similarly small-scale crime. A woman might—and did—steal a sheet on one occasion and a flat iron on another. One woman's earlier offence was fourteen days' imprisonment for stealing apples. Another woman's two offences were stealing a pair of earrings . . . one month: stealing a cheese . . . seven years' transportation. Yet another woman's two offences were both for stealing money: she served nine months for stealing one shilling and sixpence and at the age of 20 was transported for seven years for stealing £2. Finally one fifth of the Welsh women in my Tasmanian sample were regular and perhaps professional criminals.

They were by no means angels. One 27-year-old Cardiff prostitute, who was transported for stealing a watch, had already spent six months in Cardiff gaol for stealing tea and sugar and had seventeen previous convictions. Of course, these seventeen included many summary convictions for being drunk and disorderly or disturbing the peace. Another woman, also transported from Glamorgan, had eleven previous convictions for trifling offences. Despite their youth, many of these frequent offenders had accumulated and served many sentences. One Breconshire dairy maid had served the following sentences before transportation:

> Three months solitary confinement for her first offence, and thereafter two years' hard labour, one year's hard labour, six weeks and a further two year sentence, i.e. a total of nearly five and a half years.

Again these series of punishments were usually the result of a large array of small crimes. One woman's record of theft included three geese, butter and a shirt and another's consisted of bed clothes, mutton and lengths of Welsh flannel.

But not all the previous convictions were trivial, even if the crime which led to transportation was. Some previous offences included violent robberies, assaults and even manslaughter.

Despite the small minority of recidivists, the overall picture which emerges of the Welsh convict women is a sad rather than an evil one.

The women keep appearing as victims rather than villains. Some, no doubt, were fearsome and intimidating women but the harshness of the penalty inflicted upon them and even a slight understanding of their circumstances provokes a sympathetic rather than a condemnatory response in most people. Their gaolers were, of necessity, hardened people, but their proximity to the women gave them a fairly good opportunity to assess the temperament and character of their charges. A selection of their comments makes interesting reading and shows a wide variety of personalities of the women. Here are just a few:

'Has a most violent and wicked temper'
'A dissolute drunkard'
'Gaol report of the very worst kind: supposed to be very bad'
'Character, connexions, former course of life very bad'
'Quarrelsome and indolent'
'Passionate and quarrelsome'
'A very bad character'
'Disorderly, attempted suicide'
'Very indifferent'
'Light character'
'Of a very violent temper but has generally behaved, very orderly in prison: She was delivered of a female bastard child in this gaol on Saturday 20 April last, which has been removed to her settlement in Radnorshire'
'Sober and industrious but convicted before'
'A very devout woman: the chaplain speaks well of her conduct'
'Honest, industrious, giddy disposition'
'Appears a sober industrious girl: bad in the penitentiary'
'Quiet'

Revealing though the gaoler's comments are, perhaps the best way to learn about the Welsh convict women is to look at the stories of their crimes.

Chapter 4

THE CRIMES

> One day as we were a-walking
> A gentleman passed us by;
> I could see she was bent on some mischief
> By the rolling of her dark blue eye
> Gold watch she picked from his pocket
> And slyly placed into my hand:
> I was taken in charge by a copper,
> Bad luck to that black velvet band.
>
> *Chorus:* And her eyes they shone like diamonds,
> I thought her the pride of the land;
> The hair that hung down to her shoulder
> Was tied with a black velvet band.
>
> *The Girl with the Black Velvet Band*

DURING the period 1787 to 1852 when convicts were transported to New South Wales and Van Diemen's Land, there were several changes in the British penal code. The effect of these was drastically to reduce the number of offences punishable by death. Until the early nineteenth century the number of capital offences was incredibly high and included many petty offences such as picking pockets, stealing from a shop goods valued at five shillings or more, and from a house goods valued at forty shillings or more. But, in fact, even in this earlier period, transportation was very frequently substituted for the death penalty. In the 1820s Robert Peel, whose name we associate with the birth of the police force, reformed the criminal code and abolished capital punishment for many minor offences. Transportation now became the regular punishment for a wide range of crimes.

As to the offences of the female transportees, it is, perhaps, most useful to look first at general patterns of crime committed by the convict women and then to turn to individual cases. A survey carried out in Australia some years ago investigated a sample of every twentieth convict, male and female, transported from Great Britain and Ireland. Unfortunately, this sample included only thirteen Welsh women. However, its findings are very useful and it shows that British and Irish women were transported for committing the following offences.

42

Convicts in Australia, 1793
National Library of Australia

Australian Survey
Crimes committed by the Female Sample

Larceny (other than below)	587
Theft of wearing apparel	199
Robbery (so termed)	67
Receiving stolen property	52
Theft of an animal	46
Burglary or housebreaking	40
Theft, habit and repute	39
Arson. Wilful destruction	27
Coining or uttering	23
Robbery with violence	14
All other offences	44
Unknown offences	110
Total	1,248

In short, most British and Irish women were transported for a relatively small number of offences. A few points stand out from the table. By far the largest number of women were transported for some kind of theft (larceny). If one puts together those convicted of larceny, theft of wearing apparel and crimes designated as robbery, it accounts for over two-thirds of the sample. A much smaller number were transported for receiving stolen property. Also, the number convicted of burglary or housebreaking is fairly small—only 40 out of 1,248. Those charged in this table with the theft of an animal are nearly all Irish (39 out of 46) and so are those charged with arson: incendiarism reflects a particularly troubled time in Ireland's history. Violence forms only a very small part of the crimes committed by the women in the sample. Lastly, an explanation of the expression 'theft, habit and repute' may be useful. This means in the absence of conclusive evidence, a bad reputation was enough to win a person a place on an Australian transport.

How do the crimes committed by the Welsh women compare with those in the Australian sample? I have investigated and been able to discover the crimes of 179 Welsh women i.e. two out of every three Welsh female transportees.

Crimes of the Welsh Female Transportees

Larceny (other than below)	90
Theft of wearing apparel	25
Robbery (so termed)	0
Receiving stolen Property	5
Theft of an animal	13

Burglary or housebreaking   30
Theft, habit and repute   0
Arson, wilful destruction . . . . · . . .   1
Coining, uttering   3
Robbery with violence   6
All other offences   6
Unknown offences   0

                                                      Total   179

There are certain strong similarities in the two tables. The most important is that a large proportion of the crimes of the Welsh female transportees involved some sort of larceny i.e. 115 out of 179 crimes. Also, as in the Australian survey, a relatively small number were transported for receiving stolen goods. But there are some points of difference. A rather high proportion of the Welsh women were transported for burglary or housebreaking. This is not to say categorically that there were more Welsh women burglars than there were English, but one can certainly say that a higher number of Welsh women, proportionately, were transported for burglary. The actual cases of Welsh women burglars do, in fact, show the existence of gangs of women burglars and some of their escapades were very daring. Another type of crime to note in Wales is the theft of animals. It would appear that a far higher proportion of the Welsh female transportees stole animals than their English or Scottish counterparts. Only in Ireland were more women transported for this offence. Obviously, this fact reveals the rural nature of some Welsh crime. Violence does not figure prominently in women's crime, but one could note that again in Wales it seems proportionately higher than in the all-British and Irish sample of the Australian survey. That could be pure chance. But it is worth noting that there were six robberies with violence and four of the cases in the 'all other offences' column in Wales were crimes of pure violence e.g. assault and murder.

In many instances, fairly full court records survive and it is possible, to a certain extent, to reconstruct some of the crimes. It is important to see the convict women as individuals and not as statistics. The stories of their crimes are told below and are arranged in the order of the crimes given in the table.

Many of the crimes committed by the Welsh convict women took place in the urbanised areas of South Wales. The historical setting of new boom towns, closely packed housing and street violence has already been examined in a previous chapter. The background throws light on the character of some of the crimes and equally the crimes illuminate facets of Welsh life in the eighteenth and nineteenth centuries. Larceny was the commonest crime and one group of larcenies is particularly evocative of ill-lit streets, narrow bye-ways and the half world of drink and prostitution. Such crimes are designated as thefts 'from the person'. That could mean a mugging on the street or the deft removal of a watch, which the victim only later realised, or the removal of an item from someone's clothes in, for example, a lodging-house or a brothel. Often there is little detail recorded about these cases but one can state that the victims were nearly always men and that the thefts took place usually, but not exclusively, in the larger towns especially Merthyr, Cardiff and Swansea.

The following are a few cases of thefts from the person which took place in the South Wales towns. Ann Thomas, an unmarried girl of 26, was employed as a servant in Cardiff. But Ann had other ways of supplementing her income. In the Butetown area of Cardiff, which was her home area, she stole a watch and some copper coins from a man, who gave his name as John Jones. Ann was tried, found guilty and sentenced to seven years transportation by the Glamorgan court of Quarter Sessions in October 1848. But court records only give a bare outline and a lot of the actual circumstances can only be surmised. Did the theft take place on the street? It does not seem very likely that Ann, who was only 4' 11½" tall, would tackle a man in the open street. Maybe the incident took place in a brothel or low lodging house but, to be fair, Ann is not described as a prostitute. Of course, John Jones could have been drunk. Women favoured stealing from drunks and often a pair of women would approach a 'gentleman' incapacitated through drink. Henry Mayhew, who recorded the seamy side of London life, records just how pairs of women robbed drunken men and how they often used a male accomplice.

> There is another class of thieves, who steal from drunken persons, usually in the dusk of the evening, in the following manner: Two women, respectably dressed, meet a drunken man in the street, stop him and ask him to treat them. They adjourn to the bar of a public-house for the purpose of getting some gin or ale. While drinking at the bar, one of the women tries to rob him of his watch or money. A man who is called a 'stickman', an accomplice and possibly a paramour of hers, comes to the bar a short time after them. He has a glass of some kind of liquor, and stands beside them. Some motions and signs pass between the two females and this man. If they have by this time secured the booty, it is passed to the latter, who thereupon slips away, with the stolen articles in his possession.
>
> In some cases, when the property is taken from the drunken man, one of the women on some pretext steps to the door and passes it

to the 'stickman' standing outside, who then makes off with it. In other cases these robberies are perpetrated in the outside of the house, in some by-street.

Sometimes the man quickly discovers his loss, and makes an outcry against the women; when the 'stickman' comes up and asks, 'What is the matter?' the man may reply, 'These two women have robbed me.' The stickman answers, 'I'll go and fetch a policeman.' The property is passed to him by the women, and he decamps. If a criminal information is brought against the females, the stolen goods are not found in their possession, and the case is dropped.

London's Underworld

Margaret Ellis and Martha Davies, both of Cardiff, operated as a pair and stole a one pound note and four half crowns from Lewis Lewis in Cardiff. The two women were brought to trial before Glamorgan Quarter Sessions in April 1828 and were both sentenced to seven years transportation. The full story of these two is not known but a statement by Ellen Reece, a Welsh born girl, who was transported by a court in Salford in 1837, gives a few insights into thefts from the person. Speaking of her career since the age of 14, she stated

I have lived entirely by prostitution and plunder. Seven times as much by robbery as the hire of prostitution. None of the girls think so much of prostitution but as it furnishes opportunities of robbing men . . . Most girls will rob by violence and especially drunken men . . . [They] will not go to a house if they can help it; to some back Street. Gentlemen notice the features so much better when you go to a house.

Ellen Reece worked with a partner, Jane Doyle, who describes how they functioned as a team. One of the girls, having tempted the 'gentleman' into an alley, would engage his full attention: the other would pick his pocket, while his breeches were down. Both girls would run off, while the injured party was too hampered by his breeches about his ankles to pursue them. Usually the amounts of money stolen in this way were quite small but Ellen Reece knew a girl who stole £800 in this way. The irony is that that girl was acquitted!

Some Welsh women operated with male accomplices. Elizabeth James, described variously as age 27 or 34 at the time of the crime and as a red haired 'stout-made' woman, used a young man as her assistant. She committed a theft at Merthyr with the help of a young collier, named David Cross. Elizabeth James said she was a plain cook and gave her native place as Carmarthen. Both she and her collier friend were illiterate. The victim, Daniel Phillips, was described in the court record as being placed 'in danger of his life' as a result of his confrontation with James and Cross but no assault charge seems to have been brought against Elizabeth James.

There is no doubt that opportunities for theft were afforded to prostitutes. Here are just a few examples. Elizabeth Hughes, a tiny young woman (height 4′ 8″ and aged 22) with black hair and grey eyes, gave her occupation as housemaid but the Australian records make it clear she was a prostitute. She is designated as being 'on the town', for five years. The particular town in which she operated was Merthyr Tydfil. She stole a sovereign from David Powell in Merthyr and had previously been convicted of a similar offence i.e. stealing a watch. Kerziah Jones, aged 27, a dark haired woman from Butetown, Cardiff, was known to the police as a common prostitute given to disorderly behaviour. She was seventeen times summarily convicted for offences involving disorderly behaviour and prostitution. The year before her sentence of transportation to Australia, she had been picked up for disorderly conduct in Whitmore Lane and spent a month in Cardiff gaol. In 1849 she relieved Thomas Hall of two watches and the chains and for this she was transported for seven years. Mary Ann Beddow, a 21-year-old kitchen maid, who had been two years 'on the town', stole a watch from a man in Swansea in 1842. Similarly, Eleanor Watkins, a freckled and fresh complexioned dairy maid from Brecon, admitted to having been 'on the town' for eighteen months. In fact more than one town was involved. She was found guilty of thefts in Swansea and Merthyr. It was the theft from David Thomas at Merthyr which led to her being transported. Elizabeth Griffiths, a heavily tattooed woman from Swansea, stole eight shillings and sixpence from a man, called Hall, in Swansea. She gave her trade as house maid but she again admitted to having been 'on the town' for three years.

Perhaps one of the most interesting links between prostitution and theft from the person may be seen in the operation of a small gang of prostitutes who passed on their stolen property to the brothel keeper, another woman. This group operated in Glamorgan, almost certainly in Swansea. The brothel was kept by Mary Noble, a widow in her forties and the mother of six children. She stated her trade as housemaid but the gaol report on her reads, 'very bad, kept a bawdy house for many years.' She was charged and found guilty of receiving stolen property. Tried with her were three young women, of whom Mary Noble said, 'they lodged with me.' The three young women were Margaret Edwards from Swansea, aged 19, who was found guilty of stealing money from a man. She had lodged for twelve months with Mary Noble and she said that she paid one shilling and sixpence a week to live there. Secondly, Mary Williams, a farm servant from Carmarthen, aged 23, also stole from the person and the gaol report reveals the corrupting influence of

Mary Noble. Mary Williams, states the report, was 'good until acquainted with Mary Noble.' Ann Jenkin, the third woman, was somewhat older. She was 30, thickly-pockmarked and a native of Swansea. She too stole from a man and presumably passed on the goods to Mary Noble. Ann Jenkins, unlike the other women, was married but separated from her husband, who was a fisherman at Monmouth. But the whole Noble gang was rounded up. The women, sent out to commit the robberies in this Fagin-like operation, each received seven years. Mary Noble, whom the court thought directed the whole business, was sentenced to fourteen years. They all sailed to Tasmania in 1834 on board the *Edward*.

But not all thefts from the person took place in the large towns. They were committed in smaller towns such as Brecon or Monmouth. Ann Atkins, a Pembrokeshire woman, was tried for theft in Breconshire and she was described as of a bad character and 'having belonged to a gang of the worst characters.' Ann Morgan stole a silver watch, valued at sixty shillings, from a man in Presteigne, Radnorshire. Yet other such thefts took place in completely rural areas. Thomas Davies, a farmer who lived near Welshpool in Montgomeryshire, was returning home after selling his cattle at a fair in Welshpool and was carrying his proceeds with him. He tells his own story in a statement he made to the police . . .

> I reside in the village of Guildsfield in the Borough of Welchpool in this county—I came to Welchpool Fair in the Morning of Monday 16th November (1846) Instant and had there in my inside Waistcoat pocket three sovereigns and some silver—I sold two cows at the Fair for Twelve pounds ten shillings which was paid to me in gold except one Five pound bill of, I believe, the Knighton Bank in Radnorshire. I placed the money which I received at the Fair to the other money in my inside Waistcoat pocket and noticed that it was safe in my pocket when I left Pool. I started on my return home to Guildsfield between 5 and 6 o'clock, it was then getting dark, I went the road between Bryn y buckley Wood and when not far from the upper stile leading out of the wood I was overtaken by a man and a woman, the woman said to me 'Good Night' and I answered 'Good Night.' The woman again said to me 'Mr. Davies you have been very bustling today, I saw you receiving money down at the Angel.' The woman then sat down upon the side of the footpath and laid hold of the skirts of my Coat and drawed me to sit down beside her and almost immediately afterwards the man sat down upon my side, thus placing me between the two—I remained sitting down with them about 5 or 10 minutes and then got up to go away, and wished them goodnight and I

went away and also the man and woman returned in the direction of Pool. They were both dressed in dark coloured clothes and the woman had a Bonnet on. When I sat down along with them my waistcoat was properly buttoned—after I had gone a very short distance from the place where I had been sitting down I discovered that my waistcoat was unbuttoned except the lower button. I then felt my pocket inside the waistcoat and found the whole of the money about £16 was gone. I went straight home and when I arrived there I informed my son-in-law of the robbery . . . when I started from Welchpool I was quite sober.

(Signed) Thomas Davies.

His son-in-law John Richards, testified that Farmer Davies was sober on his arrival home. The day after the robbery Richards reported it to the police and then set out to pursue the woman his father-in-law had described. Acting on a tip, he went to the *Ardllin* public house. The woman, who turned out to be Eliza Thomas, a 21-year-old woman from Pool Quay, was there. She took refuge in the privy and only after a long interval did she agree to come out. She offered to return all the money she had i.e. £11, including the Knighton Bank five pound note; her accomplice had the remainder. But she was handed over to the police, brought to trial and transported to Tasmania.

One of the problems facing many of the women who stole from the person was hiding their pickings. Ellen Reece tells some of the hiding places.

The places for hiding money are pockets in the underside of the Stays towards the lower part . . . Also wrapping it in a piece of rag or paper and putting it in the hair. Also pockets inside the Stocking below the Garter. Also putting it where decency forbids to name—has known thirty Sovereigns hidden there at one time and secured. Also swallowing it—has known eleven swallowed. It has been swallowed once or twice by Girls on Deansgate beat whilst in the Lockups. Relieve themselves on the floor. If they don't get it for two or three days they get opening Medicine. Never heard of any one being injured by disposing of it either way. Has herself hid money in that way (not swallowing) perhaps thirty times. Was only three times searched there, and only once it was found. That was by the bad house woman and the Watchman, who made her jump off the Bed Stocks twice. Putting it in the Shoes another way. If a Girl heard the Constables were after her, she would swallow her money for fear—it is done regular by two or three every night almost.

1017 Morgan Sarah

Transported for Felony Record & Certain Status

Tried Glamorganshire Q. L. of Cal. ... this Offence Stealing bedding ... Roman Catholic ... 6

Embarked 1848 ... 7 Years ... reads for Mutton 18 Weeks for Flannel Married 3

Arrived 24 Sept 1849 P. Reed ... Children Sarah, Beph, Geo

Trade.	Height.	Age.	Complex.	Head.	Hair.	Whiskers.	Visage.	Forehead.	Eyebrows.	Eyes.	Nose.	Mouth.	Chin.	Native Place.
Laundress	5'¾	42	Fresh	Oval	Dark brown	—	Oval	Low	Brown	Hazel	Long	Wide	Round	South Wales

Marks A Cars on Right Cheek

Period of Gang Probation Dec 30/51 Tricklof and 2 S Hanson by Feby 1852 ...

Station of Gang

Class 3 od 19/1/52

Offences & Sentences. Nov 30/51 Rob/ Solitaire 14 days hand labor

18 P. of July 3/51 Carrg. Port. breaking according to Rev Rep. and ...

Krug formland a disorderly house / Mtts hard labor (W.G. Appt?)

1 6/51 Fault by Col 2/52 (Ksmncy) Absent v Mtts ... 9/52 Gas Colerdge/

Sept 2 9/10/51 Fault by Jang Mc51 Stealing Branch Asmarket (6m?)

Feby 18/52 Stealing Absconding Mtts hard labor 1st 52 Appn 29/3/52

Ful By 85

Larceny also includes the theft of many small items from houses or shops, but does not involve breaking and entering or burglary. Often the items stolen were of very little value. The following cases from Glamorgan will give some idea of the range and value of items taken. Mary Jenkins, tried at Glamorgan Quarter Sessions in 1792, stole 'one piece of cloth value 6d, one handkerchief, value 2d, one tortoise shell comb and case, value 1d.' Elizabeth Morgan at Merthyr stole six sauce pans, Anne Evans stole three Dutch cheeses, valued at one shilling each, Jane Isaacs stole two lengths of flannel. Sarah Morgan in Aberdare stole sheets, blankets, an ironing box, a tobacco box and one pound weight of cheese, Ann Thomas, a 15-year-old girl from Swansea, stole a measuring glass value 6d. Similarly, a few examples from other parts of Wales will demonstrate how widely the sentence of transportation was imposed for small thefts. Anne Glossop of Newtown, Montgomeryshire, stole nine yards of velvet from a shop keeper. In the same county a mother and daughter worked together. Margaret Richards, a single woman, stole a length of flannel and passed it to her mother who was transported for receiving it. Elizabeth Hughson, a 22-year-old servant stole a leg of mutton in Brecon. Another mother and daughter team, both called Elizabeth James, received sentences of fourteen years for shop lifting at Brecon Quarter Sessions in 1832 but do not appear to have sailed. In Pembrokeshire Mary Davies, a single woman of Milford, stole six yards of lace from a shop. Other transportees in Wales took bacon, printers' type, tea trays, soap, hair pins and tobacco.

By far the most common type of larceny, however, was the theft of wearing apparel. Gowns, 'dowlas' shirts, petticoats, aprons, stays, cloaks, stockings and tall Welsh beaver hats form by far the longest list of items stolen by the Welsh women convicts. Eliza Wheeler, a Herefordshire woman of 20, was employed as servant to a lady in Swansea. Eliza stole three silk shawls, value two shillings in all, from her mistress, who brought the case against her. When Loveday Lucy Cole of Llandeilo Fawr committed larceny in 1828 she stole a table cloth, handkerchiefs, six cravats and two waistcoats. Normally the stolen clothes were not of much value but an unusually high valuation was set upon the clothing taken by Ann Lewis of Dolgellau when she appeared in court in Merionethshire. She was found guilty of the theft of three hats, valued at five pounds, a shawl, valued at ten pounds, and a more humble umbrella priced at seven shillings. For this offence Ann was sentenced to fourteen years' transportation.

Another Merionethshire case involved the usual fairly low priced clothing, but the interesting point about it is the lengths to which the victim was prepared to go to retrieve her belongings. The thief was Eleanor Jones, a native of Trawsfynydd. She turned up suddenly in her home village one evening in May 1830 at about seven o'clock and obtained a bed in Mr. Davies's house. To be more accurate Eleanor was given a third of a bed, which she was to share with the daughter of the house, Elizabeth Davies, and another woman called Martha, who is simply called an inmate. Eleanor, however, rose from the bed in the middle of the night and made off with Elizabeth's hat, caps, gown and apron. Next morning her disappearance was discovered, the stolen goods were immediately missed and the nail above the latchet of the door was not in its place. Elizabeth was not prepared to put up with this. She and her father set off early in pursuit of Eleanor. They went off on foot, making inquiries as they went, and walked as far as Penrhyndeudraeth and Llanfrothen and five miles further on towards Caernarvonshire, but the search in this direction proved fruitless and about one o'clock they returned home to Trawsfynydd. By three o'clock, they were off again. This time they went in the direction of Bala, where they spent the weekend searching for the culprit, but to no avail. On Monday morning they struck out towards Dolgellau. Here they had more luck. Within half an hour of arriving in the old town, they spotted Eleanor, who was wearing the stolen clothes! Eleanor took to her heels and ran fast at the sight of the two Davies's but a police constable joined in the chase and tracked down Eleanor Jones, who was soon sentenced to seven years' transportation. Her pursuers' sixty mile hunt had paid off.

Finally, the case of Fanny Bennet involves wearing apparel and is one of the most poignant cases I have come across. Fanny, a native of Worthen, was at the age of 13, already in Montgomery gaol. Tasmanian sources reveal that she was serving a one month sentence for stealing clothing. The chaplain of the gaol, the Rev. J. Lloyd, and the rector of Llanmerewig took pity on Fanny. They found her a job in the rectory at Llanmerewig. Fanny, who was a small girl with grey eyes and sandy hair, took up her duties as a housemaid. She had previously been living with her mother and one brother and sister: there is no reference to a father. Her new post was, of course, residential. But Fanny obviously did not like her new job at the rectory. She had begun work on 28 July, but less than one month later, on the morning of 19 August, 1848, she was missing. Fanny had absconded. She took with her various items of clothing from the rectory, namely one recently purchased black whittle, two small shawls and an umbrella. Fanny did not get far. She was tracked down by a policeman, brought to trial and transported to Tasmania.

Many other larceny cases involved theft from shops. Women wearing voluminous dresses and sometimes carrying muffs had plenty of places to hide stolen goods. Jane Reece, the Welsh girl, who turned to a life of crime in Liverpool, gives plenty of insights into the nineteenth-century shoplifter's art. Whilst in prison she was asked, 'When not in honest

employment, how were you maintained?' She replied, 'Shoplifting—
Bad Houses. Generally went two together. Shoplifting—method was to
go into a linen drapers shop, first rate shops, and ask to see linen at such
a price. Ask for Lute-string and take a bit for a pattern, take a yard of
lute-string and 2 or 3 yards of linen, then ask for Stocking, Gloves,
Handkerchiefs, and when a good many things on the counter, so that
they did not know the Count of them, when the back was turned to
reach something else, to slip them under their shawl; sometimes into a
large square fustian pocket fastened round the waist and hanging nearly
to the knees. This is not a very common thing—she and Margaret Axon
(who is transported) made it out themselves. Paid for the small articles
and walked out gently and made away as fast as they could to Newton
Lane; a person of the name of Thompson who kept a private house in
Thompson Street, Newton Lane, he was what is called "a Fence" he
was taken up 3 years ago transported for 14 years. After he was gone
could not find anyone else to take 'em and thought it dangerous to go to
pawnbrokers, so gave over Shoplifting and took entirely to the Streets
and robbing Mens pockets. Made a deal of money Shoplifting, made £1
each in the day . . . She did not become a regular prostitute 'till Shoplifting failed—was miserable both ways, but going on the Streets was
most profitable . . .' But goods could be removed from shops in yet
more subtle ways. Margaret Williams, a 24-year-old woman from St.
Mellons, Monmouthshire, appeared before the Glamorgan Court of
Great Sessions in the spring of 1814. She was charged with a whole
series of incidents in which she obtained goods by false pretences. Her
method was simply to enter a shop and then pose as the wife of some
prosperous and credit-worthy gentleman. She took the goods away with
her, leaving the account to be settled later. The court record, given
below, charts her progress around the shops at Cardiff. The following
all happened in one day!

> Margaret Griffiths . . . charged upon the oath of Alice Jones, the
> wife of Thomas Jones, of the Town of Cardiff, Draper, with
> having on the third day of March instant obtained from the said
> Alice Jones, by the said Margaret Griffiths, representing herself to
> be the wife of Evan David, of the Little Mill at Ely and by other
> false pretences the following goods, the property of the said
> Thomas Jones; that is to say, Seven Yards of Dowlas, at 2 shillings
> per yard. Five yards and a half of Black Bombazett at 2s. 4d. per
> yard, three yards and a quarter of Green Beaver at 14 shillings per
> yard, one yard of brown Holland at 18d a yard, a quantity of Sew-
> ing Silks at 2 shillings, a quantity of Thread at 2½d., Three Muslin
> Handkerchiefs at 2s. 4d. each, one dozen large bone moulds at 3d.
> per dozen, one dozen of the same sort of 2d., one pair of leather

gloves at 2s. 6d., one pair of muslin gloves at 1s. 6d. two earthen jugs at 1/- each, one large oval dish at 1s., two small dishes at 8d. each and three pennyworth of Twist.

Also charged upon the oath of John Davies Bird, of the town of Cardiff, Bookseller, with having on the third day of March instant, obtained from him by falsely and deceitfully representing herself to be the wife of David Roberts of Rumney, in the county of Monmouth and by other false pretences, the following goods, that is to say, One Pair of Worsted and Leather Men's Braces, at 2s. 6d., one yard of Black Silk at 8s. 6d., One Leather Thread lace at 1/-, one Yard and a half of Thread Lace at 6s. 6d. per yard, a quantity of Sewing Silk and Iron Bodkin at 3d. One Ivory Small Tooth Comb at 8d., Two pieces of Linen Tape at 1s. 6d., One Iron and Horn penknife at 6d., Two Black Worsted Stay laces at 2d. and a quantity of Brass pins and Wire, and Thread Buttons at 10d.

Also charged upon the oath of Henry Partridge, of the town of Cardiff, Ironmonger, with having on the third day of March instant, obtained from him by falsely and deceitfully, representing herself to be the wife of Morgan Williams of Dynaspowis, and by other false pretences the following Goods, the property of his Father, Samuel Partridge, Ironmonger, that is to say One Tea Tray at 10s. 6d., One Tin Japan Tea Caddy, at 4s. 6d. and One Brass and Iron Toaster at 5/-.

One might also note that some of the larceny cases had a distinctly rural character and the theft of farm produce set a small group of Welsh women on the road to Australia. Mary James, a 29-year-old woman and her companion, Catherine Jenkins, aged 54, were charged upon the oath of John Jenkins of Llantwit Major, Glamorgan, of breaking into his barn and stealing a quantity of 'wheat in the chaff', value forty shillings. The two women appeared before the court of Great Sessions in 1808 and confessed their crime. Both were sentenced to transportation but the older woman did not actually sail. The explanation for this, I am convinced, lies less in concern for an older woman than in the uselessness in Australia of a 54-year-old woman as an object of sexual gratification for free males and male convicts.

In Pembrokeshire, Sophia Jones of the parish of Wiston was charged in 1801 with stealing wheat, oat meal and barley from a house. For this she was sentenced to transportation for Life. It is relevant to note that 1801 was a year of terrifically high prices. Prices were at famine level, wheat in 1801 costing 115s. 11d. per quarter, or more than double its normal value. Whether Sophia's action forms part of a more general outburst in Pembrokeshire against such high prices or whether it was a solitary crime to relieve the condition of her own family is not known. But I think this crime is probably very directly related to acute poverty, aggravated by the peculiarly high prices of a difficult period.

The theft of bread, cheese, bacon and meat was common among the convict women. I believe that these items were taken to feed themselves and their children and not for resale. Just a few examples will serve:

> Elizabeth Jenkins was transported for 15 years by Monmouth Assizes for stealing bacon and 7s. 6d. in money in 1841.

> Ann Roberts of Pembroke town was transported for stealing a basket of veal at the town market.

> Ellen Davies, a 19-year-old Brecon girl, was convicted in Anglesey of stealing bacon and a loaf. She does not appear to have committed any previous offence.

Even the theft of apples or cherries from gardens earned people prison sentences in these years.

Four cabbages were the immediate cause of one Merionethshire widow's transportation to the Australian penal colonies. Ruth Roberts was caught in the yard of the *Goat*, Bala, by Evan Evans, a servant at the inn. He recognised her and entreated her to step forward out of the darkness. 'Ruth, come from there, for shame', he said. As she moved, the cabbages fell and rolled along the ground. She entreated Evan Evans on her hands and knees to let her go and not tell anybody. But he did and the police constable took her off to the house of correction. Then the detective work commenced. The cabbages were found to fit and match exactly four headless stalks in the garden of Dr. Owen Richards. The case against Ruth was conclusive. She already had previous offences, including stealing a seemingly useless pair of clockmaker's cutting nippers, and she must have realised that the sentence of transportation was almost inevitable.

There are two interesting cases which involve thefts from waggons or coaches. One took place in Carmarthenshire and concerned a woman called Sarah Smith. Her case is somewhat unusual. Tired and hot, she was returning with her child on a summer's day from Carmarthen to Llandeilo when she hitched a lift from William Davies, the driver of the waggon of Messrs. North and Morgan, Carriers. Davies demanded payment for the ride and on discovering she had no money, proposed in the words of the court record, 'an illicit connection'. Sarah obliged and in return for her favours, Davies gave Sarah 50 yards of 'Cloth called Huckabuck' from his employer's wagon. Sarah's crime came to light when she tried to sell the cloth. Mr. North wrote from Brecon to Miss Morgan at Llandeilo, 'as to the woman, I would have you take her before a magistrate who will of course commit her to Gaol—and you may be sure she will tell the truth regarding W. Davies who deserves to be hanged.' In vengeful vein he continued, 'I trust you will do all in your power to get the woman punished also.' In fact, Sarah Smith was transported for seven years to New South Wales!

A second instance of theft from a waggon which led to a sentence of transportation for the female thief took place in Caernarvonshire. Benjamin Williams of Chester was a driver in the employment of James Williams of Holyhead. He was driving the waggon towards Chester but stopped overnight in Bangor. In a written statement, he said that he had left his waggon overnight on Monday 1 October 1811 in a yard opposite the Cathedral Church. He went off to the *Mitre Inn* at Bangor for his lodgings but he left certain luggage, which was to be taken on to Chester in the waggon, i.e. three boxes, one trunk and one hamper. At five o'clock next morning, after dealing with his horses, he went to the waggon. On reaching his waggon, he found the boxes broken into and empty. His statement continued, that he was 'led to believe' that Ann Parry, alias Jones, a common prostitute, was the guilty party. The person who had pointed his finger at Ann Parry was John Lewis, a Bangor chaise and coach driver, employed by the keeper of the inn at Bangor.

John Lewis told how on the night of the robbery he had taken his master's horses to the field for the night. On his way he heard a woman's voice say, 'Nanny, you had better come out of the way as the horses are coming from the stables.' In fact, Nanny, or Ann, was in Benjamin Williams' waggon. John Lewis soon had confirmation of her presence. She invited him to join her saying, 'Will you come to me, dear Jack?' But he replied somewhat bluntly, 'No, you have but a poor lodging tonight', and went on tending to his horses. But even after Benjamin Williams had received this information from John Lewis, he had to actually catch Ann. She had fled the mainland and crossed by the Garth Ferry to Anglesey. Acting on reports of 'a woman carrying a bundle across Garth Ferry', Benjamin Williams pursued her. He found her coming out of a small house just half a mile away from the ferry on the Anglesey side. She put up no pretence. She was holding the bundle when he found her. When he asked where the stolen goods were, she replied bluntly, 'These are them.' The bundle contained two beaver hats, one woman's black gown, one pelice, three gross of coat buttons and one coach lamp without glass. Ann Parry, alias Jones, was tried at Caernarvonshire Court of Great Sessions in the following March. She was sentenced to seven years' transportation.

There are only a few cases of Welsh women being transported for receiving stolen goods. Mary Noble's nefarious operation has already been mentioned. Ann Driffield, a widow, appeared at Monmouth Assizes in 1844 and was found guilty of receiving knives and forks. Mary Jenkins appeared at Monmouth Court of Quarter Sessions in

1849 and was found guilty of buying stolen herrings and potatoes. She does not appear to have ever been convicted of any other offence. One tends to think of receiving as a woman's crime but there are several cases of a woman committing the theft and a man being found guilty of receiving. In Anglesey, Mary Lewis of the parish of Pentraeth, committed a robbery. She and her husband, John Lewis, a labourer, fled to Holywell in Flintshire. The charge brought against John Lewis was receiving the goods, which Mary had stolen.

Receiving was punished quite severely. Ann Driffield was given a fourteen year sentence and Mary Jenkins a ten year sentence. This compares with seven years as a very common sentence for most larcenies. Ann Jones, a native of Tickley, was charged with receiving a stolen horse. She appeared before Radnorshire Assizes in 1835 and although she seemed to have no earlier criminal record, she was sentenced to transportation for life. The explanation for the severity of this sentence is no doubt because the stolen property was an animal.

The theft of animals was not an infrequent crime among the Welsh female transportees. Although most crimes do appear to be urban, this type of crime reminds one of the rural nature of some Welsh crime. Margaret Davies, alias Mary Jones, of Llangyvelach, Glamorgan, appeared before the Glamorgan Court of Great Sessions in the autumn of 1801. She had stolen a black cow with a speckled face value £5 and sold it. But, if this was not enough, she had committed a second offence of stealing another cow on the same day.

But, not surprisingly, most animal thefts in Wales were of sheep. The theft of sheep was considered a very serious crime and was punished extremely severely. In Caernarvonshire Mary Williams and Mary, the wife of Robert Roberts, a labourer, both of Llaniestyn, stole two wether sheep, valued at 10 shillings each. From the evidence of witnesses, this appears a somewhat violent crime. The two women were seen one foggy winter afternoon at 4.00 p.m. entering a field near Caerain in the parish of Llaniestyn. They caught two sheep, killed them and cut off their ears—no doubt bearing the owner's mark. One sheep was bundled into Mary William's cloak and the carcase of the other was put into a pannier. When questioned, Mary Williams admitted taking and killing 'one small ewe', but her companion only confessed to accepting a small piece of mutton. Quite how seriously the court viewed sheep stealing is seen by the sentence passed on the two women. Both were transported for life.

In the late eighteenth century Catherine Williams of Breconshire was found guilty of sheep stealing. In 1789 she was sentenced to death but, fortunately for her, the sentence was commuted to seven years' transportation to New South Wales. Some years later in the same county, Margaret Jones and a male companion stole five wether sheep. They drove them into Brecon town, where they tried to sell them at a guinea a head but quickly and, perhaps, suspiciously dropped the price to fifteen shillings. Their behaviour in Brecon was noticed and when they entered the *Bear Inn* they were recognised and chased. Margaret and the sheep, which she drove in front of her, were caught. The man apparently escaped. Margaret was sentenced to transportation for life, as were the two Caernarvonshire women cited above. In the case of all these women there is no evidence of any previous convictions.

Perhaps the case of sheep stealing dealt with most severely of all took place in Carmarthenshire. Charlotte Williams differs in many respects from other Welsh convict women. Firstly, she was 54-years-old when she was tried in Carmarthenshire Assizes and she was 56 on arrival in Van Diemen's Land. She gave her occupation as a dairy-woman. She was married and was the mother of nine children. There is no evidence that she had committed any previous offences. She was charged and found guilty of sheep stealing. For this offence she was sentenced to fourteen years' transportation. The horror of this case lies in the fact that, along with Charlotte were tried her husband James and three of her sons for the same offence. They were all transported. Her other six children were left behind.

In Caernarvonshire two members of another family were transported together. They were two sisters, both 'servants in husbandry' and both described as of 'light character'. Elizabeth Jones was aged 17 and her sister Catherine was 34. Again, neither of these two was a previous offender and yet both were given life sentences.

The other type of livestock stolen by the women is poultry. Ann Griffiths in Breconshire, Mary Bevans in Pembrokeshire, and Elizabeth Thomas in Caernarvonshire all stole poultry. But none of these received a life sentence. Seven years for stealing a chicken or a goose is a heavy enough sentence!

Somewhat surprisingly, none of the Welsh women convicts appear to have been convicted as poachers. Maybe this was not their line or maybe they were very good at it. Cases of burglary or breaking-and-entering account for many convictions of the Welsh women convicts. The legal distinction between the two offences is that burglary takes place at night and breaking and entering in the day-light hours. Both types of crime occurred in all areas of Wales, both urban and rural.

Mary Griffiths of Montgomeryshire was charged with three offences committed within a week in June 1801. To all three charges she pleaded not guilty. Two charges concerned her breaking into an inn in the town of Montgomery and removing goods from there. She crept in at night while the servant dozed before the fire and stole a piece of bacon. The bacon was found in Mary's pocket and carefully fitted into the whole flitch where it was found to match perfectly! Mary also stole clothing which belonged to a servant girl at the inn. But the third charge brought against her involved an incident which took place a few days later and was not a charge of breaking and entering but simply of larceny. Mary had taken lodgings at Llanwyddelan in the home of the Evans family. She shared a room and a bed with the daughter of the house, Catherine. On Sunday night the two girls went to bed at ten o'clock but at 3.00 a.m. Catherine awoke to find Mary 'missing from bed' and her own clothes stolen.

Some women burglars went in for large hauls. The case of Charlotte Davies is really quite amazing. Charlotte, of Llangystennin in Caernarvonshire, entered the house of Elizabeth Davies. No one was in at the time and her house was in a lonely position. Elizabeth had locked up the house and left the key with her next door neighbour, some distance away. Charlotte broke in through a window and absolutely cleared the house of its contents apart from the furniture! She took:

2 pairs of stockings	value 6d.
1 woollen petticoat	6s. 0d.
2 shifts	2s. 0d.
1 pair of fustian pockets	6d.
1 Stuff bedgown	1s. 0d.
1 woollen bedgown	1s. 0d.
1 Stuff gown	10s. 0d.
2 cotton handkerchieves	6d.
3 silk handkerchieves	3s. 0d.
1 felt bonnet	2s. 0d.
1 peck of wheat	6s. 0d.
1 cotton quilt	10s. 0d.
3 muslin caps	2s. 0d.
2 stuff aprons	6s. 0d.
1 check apron	6s. 0d.
1 pair of cotton stays	1s. 0d.
1 piece of bacon ham	2s. 0d.
3 pounds of soap	1s. 0d.
1 pair black silk gloves	6d.
1 pound of blue woollen yarn	2s. 0d.
1 silk parasol	2d.
1 cotton workbag	2d.
1 silk handkerchief	1s. 0d.
2 pieces of linen cloth	1s. 0d.

Charlotte must have been quite laden as she made her escape. Her activities in disposing of all her loot came to light and a number of witnesses testified.

A woman called Catherine Jones was given a bonnet by Charlotte and Charlotte told her it came from an aunt. But the victim of the robbery, Elizabeth Davies, was doing her own detective work and came round to Catherine Jones' house looking for Charlotte and asking if Charlotte was selling clothes. She saw the bonnet which Catherine had just acquired. 'It is mine', she said and took it. Catherine Jones' family had done rather well out of Charlotte's robbery. Catherine's mother had received a stuff apron and her sister the work bag and the parasol. Charlotte had also sold Mrs. Jones a quantity (fioled) of wheat. Whether Charlotte had actually given these things away, as the new owners affirmed, or whether she sold them is not certain: possibly, they did not like admitting to having purchased what was pretty obviously stolen property. Anyone who knew Charlotte and her difficult circumstances would realise she did not own all this clothing. A further witness, called Jane Davies, came forward. Charlotte had tried to sell her a stolen petticoat. During this transaction Charlotte had said that she was 'just famished with hunger.' It is one of the very few surviving statements made by one of the female transportees which throws light on the motive for crime. That Charlotte was obviously very poor is apparent from two other pieces of evidence. When Jane Davies asked Charlotte where she had acquired the petticoat, she had replied 'from the parish.' Even more indicative of the poverty of Charlotte is the statement by the victim Elizabeth Davies. She explained why she suspected Charlotte in the first place. 'I suspected Charlotte Davies having broken open my house because she was a woman of ill fame, having heard she had been accused of stealing before and she is said to wander about sleeping at nights in hovels and houses.'

Another story of a house breaker who was obviously very poor is that of a Pwllheli woman, Jane Griffiths. Jane broke into the bedroom of a house at Brynadda, in the parish of Bangor. Similarly, she was caught out when she tried to sell the old clothing which she had stolen. Jane seems to have tried selling the clothes to anyone who would buy. She approached one woman and offered to sell her a linseed apron for ninepence. But this woman did not possess ninepence—at least so she told Jane. The woman offered Jane food for the apron and Jane was only too glad to accept it. A little later, Jane was to be seen selling another stolen garment—this time a shawl. Jane did not even attempt to raise money for the shawl but offered it to a buyer in exchange for bread. She actually got part of a loaf. It is quite clear that Jane was no big-time criminal, nor even a successful small-time robber. She was desperately poor. When she came to dispose of a final item of clothing, another shawl, she simply said to a would-be purchaser, 'I am in want of meat.'

The case of Alice Williams shows a housebreaker who was full of plausible explanations of how she came to possess a long list of stolen clothing. Alice, a single woman of the parish of Whitchurch in the county of Glamorgan, was charged with stealing clothing from the house of one Edmund Lewis the Younger at Whitchurch near Cardiff. The list included a linen gown, a petticoat, a shawl, a handkerchief, a dowlas shirt, a hat, a check apron and a flannel apron. When cross-examined at the court of Great Sessions, Alice had an answer for everything. Where had she got the hat? The hat, she maintained, her father had bought in Bristol. The petticoat . . . where had she got that? Alice said she had bought that in Mrs. William's shop in Cardiff twelve months ago. The flannel apron? Where did that come from? Her sister, according to Alice, had given her the yarn for that and it had been woven up for her by a weaver called William Rees. And the check apron? Alice had bought that at Mrs. Vaughan's shop in Caerphilly at the end of the previous April. And the shawl? This shawl, which was purple and white, was the gift of Alice's old mistress Mrs. William Williams of St. Fagan's. And the linen gown? That too was from Mrs. Vaughan's shop in Caerphilly. The yellow and white handkerchief? Alice said that her father had given her that in exchange for another handkerchief. Finally, the dowlas shirt? Alice said she had bought that at Mrs. William's shop in Cardiff. The court did not believe Alice and she was transported, but her detailed defence gives a remarkable picture of the wide range of shopping centres used by one woman.

A case where the female burglar actually broke her way in, took place in Cornelly. Ann David, aged 19, of North Cornelly also in Glamorgan, together with Margaret the wife of Thomas Beynon, who had moved into the area from Llansamlet, were accused and found guilty of burglary. In 1797 they were charged with breaking into a small shop at Cornelly. The shop belonged to a woman called Cecil(y) Williams. Cecily obviously sold practically everything because her list of stolen goods included:

50 yards ribband	Value	10s. 0d.
2 ozs. of black silk		4s. 6d.
6 dozen buttons		4s. 6d.
2 dozen stay laces		1s. 6d.
1 oz. thread		2d.
1 piece tape		5d.
4 muslin handkerchieves		8s. 0d.
1 yard calincano [sic.]		10d.
1 yard cotton		2s. 0d.
¼ yard striped cotton		6d.
2 yards muslin		1s. 0d.

3 lbs. weight of pigtail tobacco	9s. 0d.
16 pair of black tin buckles	8s. 0d.
1 oz. snuff	3d.
20 pieces of copper coin (called halfpence)	10d.
3 lbs. butter	1s. 10½d.
2 combs	3d.

A number of witnesses made statements before the justices regarding this case. One woman witness said that she had noticed something amiss on her way to work: the shop door was wide open. Cecily's sister, Margaret, a spinster, also made a statement. She had been alerted to the open shop door by the first witness and when she came down stairs she perceived, 'about seven paines of glass had been broken in the window and that the door which adjoins to the window frame, on the lane side, had been unbolted on the inside apparently by a hand through the broken window.' She quickly noticed the theft. Margaret, somewhat unusually, signed her statement: no doubt, she helped Cecily with the books. The local constable, John Hopkin, made his statement. He was illiterate and merely added his mark to the document. He had found goods in the house of William Beynon and Margaret, his wife, confessed to receiving them between 10 and 11 p.m. on Tuesday night from Ann David. Ann was brought in and confessed all.

Although Ann David had stolen a long list of items they would have been quite light and therefore easily portable but some of the female transportees stole enormous weights. The case of Maria Jones of Trefeglwys in Montgomeryshire who broke into a house in the same county and made off with a very heavy load will illustrate this. Acting apparently without assistance, she stole:

4 cheeses	Value	10s. 0d.
40 lbs. weight of cheese		10s. 0d.
3 lbs. weight of tallow		1s. 0d.
½ peck wheaten flour		2s. 0d.
10 quarts wheaten flour		2s. 0d.
10 quarts other flour		2s. 0d.

Quite a large number of burglaries took place in Carmarthenshire and there is evidence of the operation of female gangs there.

Elizabeth Davies, spinster of the parish of Llangendeirne, was one of a small gang which robbed three houses at Llangendeirne, Llanon and Lanarthney within the space of four days in early June 1791. Their haul was mainly clothing—aprons, stockings, handkerchiefs and felt hats. For these crimes Elizabeth was sentenced to death. This sentence was commuted to transportation for life.

Another gang of Carmarthenshire women acted with great aplomb. The case of Ann Lloyd, age 25, better known to her associates as Nanny, and Martha Daniel (alias David), age 26, both single women of Llansadwrn, is remarkable. Together with two other women associates, one night they burgled the house of Robert Jones, Victualler, at Maesgoden in the parish of Llansadwrn. Their tracks away from the house remained visible in the snow of that January night and the turnpike keeper at Abermarlais recognised the woman who had ridden on a stolen horse, carrying something under her cloak, as Martha Daniel: she had, he said, been 'saucey' to him. There followed the arrest of all four women and all told totally different tales. Martha, who may have organised the crime, had in fact been previously employed as a servant in the victualler's house: she denied all knowledge of the incident. Nanny Lloyd, however, confessed to the theft and said it was the idea of Martha and one of the other women. She said that they had feasted on the victualler's salmon and bread, stolen his candlesticks and saucepans and a large quantity of tallow, the last of which they had hidden in a pig-sty. Acting on this, the constable found the stolen goods. The four were tried at Great Sessions and a sentence of transportation for life was passed on all of them. Nothing more is heard of the other two women and it seems likely that they never sailed. Of course, there is a clue why these two women did not sail. Emma Griffiths was 46 and Mary Evans was 35. Compare these with the ages of Nanny at 25 and Martha at 26. The two older women could be of far less 'use' in Australia.

In Anglesey another gang of housebreakers operated. This was mainly a male gang but it contained one woman, Jessie White, from Airdrie in Scotland. She was sentenced at Beaumaris in 1850 along with five men, who were transported for the same offence.

A final Carmarthenshire burglary case provoked a very bold response from the victim. Hannah Williams, spinster of Llangunnor, in May 1800 broke into the house of Sarah Jenkin near Goed Gaing between 11.00 a.m. and 1.00 p.m. while Sarah was working at a neighbour's house. On her return, Sarah found 'the bar of the lock broke and the door nearly half open.' Rushing to her chest, she discovered the theft of her flannel apron and of two handkerchiefs belonging to a male servant, who also lived in the house. She hastened in pursuit of the thief and learnt locally that a woman had been seen going towards Llanddarog with a pack on her back. At a farm called Penygraig in the parish of Llanon, Sarah overtook and challenged Hannah, who was still holding the stolen goods. This incident led to the arrest and sentence of seven years' transportation for Hannah.

Cardiganshire's only female transportee, Eleanor James, was committed for housebreaking. She appeared before Thomas Lewis Lloyd,

Sheriff, at the Court of Great Sessions held at Cardigan on 2 September 1822. According to the Calendar of Prisoners, Eleanor James, age 24, was charged with feloniously stealing from the house of a certain Anne Thomas in the little village of Tremain. She allegedly removed one gown, one silk shawl and one handkerchief, the property of one Mary Phillips, and one cloak, petticoat, silk handkerchief and flannel apron, the property of Anne Thomas. David George, age 59, was charged with removing a similar array of clothing from the same house. In the absence of detailed evidence, it is not possible to reconstruct the crime, but it would seem that David George was found in possession of the stolen goods. He was apprehended in early May, whilst Eleanor James was not brought in and charged until July.

The crime of arson seems to have been committed by only one Welsh woman transportee. Eleanor Williams, a 31-year-old Carmarthenshire farm servant, was found guilty of setting fire to a house. There are no clues as to why she did it. This could be a story of jealousy or personal hatred. On the other hand it may be of greater social consequence and may mask some social or political protest. Eleanor, we know, was a widow with a very young baby. The baby, aged 8 months, sailed with her.

A few Welsh women were charged with forgery. Sarah Chandler of 'The Dolly', Presteigne, Radnorshire, appeared before the court of Great Sessions in Easter 1814. She was charged with forgery, found guilty and sentenced to death. The full details of the case are not known but there are clearly some alarming features to this case. Sarah was granted bail in April 1813—a full year before her case was heard. The bail was very high indeed—£100—and no doubt the money was carefully examined! The granting of bail is a very rare occurrence with these women and I suspect that this is the only instance of it among the female transportees. It suggests that Sarah was a woman of some means. Three years after her trial at Great Sessions Sarah is to be found listed among prisoners in Radnor gaol! At some point, after the verdict in 1814, her sentence of death was changed to transportation for life. She sailed on the *Friendship* in June 1817 and arrived in New South Wales in 1818, four years after being apprehended.

It is a strange coincidence that Margaret Jones of Denbighshire, another forger, also sailed on the same ship. Margaret Jones was found guilty of eleven instances of forging bank notes. The offence of 'coining' was also committed by one convict woman. Mary Smith, an elderly Irish woman, was tried and found guilty, along with her husband, for this offence. They were tried at Caernarvon.

Clearly, the overwhelming majority of the crimes committed by the Welsh women convicts were against property. The Australian survey, mentioned at the beginning of this chapter, shows that an astounding

Denbighshire to wit. The Jurors for our sovereign Lord the King upon their Oath present that Margaret Jones late of Denbigh in the County of Denbigh heretofore to wit on the Twelfth day of November in the Fifty seventh year of the reign of our Sovereign Lord George the Third by the Grace of God of the United Kingdom of Great Britain and Ireland King Defender of the Faith with force and arms at Denbigh — in the County of Denbigh feloniously knowingly and willingly and without lawful excuse had in her possession and custody divers forged and counterfeited Bank Notes that is to say One forged and counterfeited Bank Note the tenor of which said forged and counterfeited Bank Note is as followeth that is to say

Felony

Bank of England 1816

No 91782 to pay to Mr Henry Hase No 91782

on Demand the Sum of One Pound

ONE

1816 Augt 11 London 11 Augt 1816.

For the Govr and Compa
of the Bank of England

One

83% of women convicts had committed crimes against property and only 1% against the person. The figure for male convicts is only a little different, i.e. 81% against property as against 3% against the person.

Violence had only a small part to play in the crimes of the Welsh women. A handful of crimes against property of some description involved violence. Mary Davies, a Merthyr laundress, was charged with highway robbery with violence. She appeared, together with a man, before Glamorgan Quarter Sessions in 1841. The details are lost but we know the amount involved was only 8s. 6d. in silver and coppers. It is always difficult to appreciate the value of money in other ages but suffice it to say that a widow and three children were expected to live on 10s. a week in the 1850s, at least that is what they got on poor relief. Obviously, the case was regarded as serious and Mary was given the comparatively rare fifteen-year sentence. But Mary was hardly an Amazon to terrorise the streets. She was 5 feet 2 inches and had no criminal record, but the gaol report called her 'a common prostitute of the lowest kind.' Female highway robbers were quite unusual but not unknown. In 1785 Mary Pile, age 20, appeared at the Old Bailey. She was described in its records as Mary Pile, 'the female highwayman.'

A few other crimes of Welsh women were variously described as 'assault with intent to rob' or 'robbery with violence'. Ann Lee and Ann Pike were charged at Monmouth in 1829 of assault with intent to rob. Both were in their 20's and both came from England, i.e. from Shrewsbury and Southampton respectively. Ann Lee called herself a housemaid and Ann Pike a dressmaker. The details of their attack and robbery are not known but both women were given very bad reports by their gaoler. They are described as 'of the very worst kinds, connexions supposed very bad.' One feature suggesting toughness about Ann Lee are her tattoos. She was the woman who bore a tattoo on her right arm of a heart and on her left arm the design of a jug, a bottle and H.O.P.E. Both were sentenced to seven years' transportation and they sailed together on the *Eliza* to Tasmania.

A number of robberies with violence took place in Glamorgan in the early 1850s. Elizabeth Smith, a tiny woman, height 4 feet 9¼ inches was described as having a 'most violent and wicked temper and is of the very worst kind of prostitute.' Her victim was a woman called Mrs. Riddle whom she attacked and robbed. Two other women charged with similar offences were Mary Ann Powhill and Mary Williams. Both were Monmouthshire women but were tried at Glamorgan Assizes. In fact, Mary Williams really had travelled to the capital of crime and had previous convictions in London.

As regards crimes of violence solely against the person, there are very few of these but what cases there were, are sometimes quite spectacular. Ann Thomas, a 31-year-old single woman, together with a sailor,

447 Powhill Mary Ann

Transported for																

Tried _Chronister of Assizes 27 February_

Embarked _1851_ — 7 years

Arrived _16 January 1852_

Trade.	Height.	Age.	Complex.	Head	Hair.	Whiskers.	Visage.	Forehead	Eyebrows.	Eyes.	Nose.	Mouth.	Chin.	Native Place.
Maid	_5 2_	_26_	_Dark_	_Round_	_Brown_	_—_	_Oval_	_Middling_	_Brown_	_Brown_		_Middling_		_Newport_

Marks _M of R of A under lower lip and W M A Pepper ? part right arm_

Period of Gang Probation

Station of Gang

Class

Offences & Sentences.

Remarks.

State Library of Tasmania

The record shows that Mary Ann Powhill of Newport was transported for robbery with violence

Jeremy Williams, was charged with having 'feloniously assaulted a police constable with attempt to do him grievous bodily harm.' The incident took place in Swansea and Ann got seven years as a result of it.

A case of extreme violence, involving a husband and wife, occurred in Carmarthenshire in the 1830s and was brought before the Assizes in 1834. Sarah Gunter, a stout, dark, 31-year-old woman from Stoke-on-Trent and her husband, David, a tin man, were both transported as a result of a brawl. The cause of the fight was a third party, a man who insulted and attacked Sarah. The episode is best related in Sarah's own words.

> A man was struck by my Husband with a Soldering Iron for knocking me down under a cart wheel. I had first smacked his face for using impudent language to me.

Sarah was found guilty of 'malicious cutting' and she and David were both sentenced to seven years' transportation. According to Sarah, David, found guilty of the same offence, sailed first. It is really difficult to know the truth here. Was David protecting his wife? Who was the other man? What social class did the other man belong to? One detail throws a little light. In later years Sarah, who had been offended by impudent language in this case, was found guilty of indecent language, threats and assault!

There are two far more serious crimes of violence: Mary Jones, a Caernarvonshire dairy maid in her twenties, is described as a fresh faced girl with a ruddy complexion and freckles. Her crime was murdering her bastard child. The actual charge was manslaughter. When one considers that Mary Jones was a Baptist and that she lived in a small North Walian community, it is not difficult to imagine the shame which she brought upon herself by having an illegitimate baby. In fact, Mary had never previously committed any crime and her behaviour was described as good. But the surprising thing about this case of infanticide is that this was not a new-born baby. There are many horrific tales of Welsh servant girls, who became pregnant, and were terrified of losing their jobs. They tried hard to conceal their pregnancies and often gave birth in secret in attics and cellars. They then smothered the new born baby. But Mary Jones' case was not like this. She killed her baby when it was already six-months-old. We just cannot know the personal stresses behind this awful act, but a strongly disapproving community must take its share of the blame.

The final case which I want to single out is the only murder I have come across. Normally, one expects a murderer at this period to be hanged, but there were obviously mitigating circumstances in Hannah Roberts' case. It was clearly a 'crime of passion'. Hannah Roberts of Holywell, Flintshire, was a short, hazel-eyed, round faced girl of 18 and she gave her occupation as housemaid. She is described as supposedly honest and industrious, but of a giddy disposition and hasty. She too had never committed a criminal offence before. Hannah was married, but this did not prevent her from having an affair with another man. The other man, who was called John Parry, became her lover and the father of her child. But John Parry was not satisfied with this arrangement and wanted to do away with Hannah's husband. Parry gave Hannah arsenic with which to poison her husband. Hannah said in her statement that she did not know what it was. Anyway, she put it in her husband's dinner! He, poor man, was soon aware of its toxic properties and he clung to life for a whole week after taking the arsenic. Hannah was sentenced at Flint Assizes in 1842 to be hanged but the sentence was commuted to transportation for life.

In conclusion, one can say that the crimes of the Welsh convict women were nearly all crimes against property. Theft of some kind accounts for the transportation of most of the Welsh women convicts. Often—but not always—the amounts involved were very small and the single item most taken was worn clothing. The limited character of female crime reflects in many ways their restricted life styles. They simply lacked the opportunities of male convicts to steal from wider pastures, for example, collieries or dockyards or railways. When women stole from their employers they were working as household servants and so they took the familiar items of clothing and household linen. But not quite all female crime fits into this pattern. The operation of highly organised gangs of female burglars and the theft of animals by women suggests a more independent breed of women convicts than has usually been supposed.

Chapter 5

THE CAUSES OF CRIME

> You lads and lasses all attend to me
> While I relate my tale of misery;
> By hopeless love was I once betrayed,
> And now I am, alas, a Convict Maid.
>
> To please my lover did I try so sore,
> That I spent upon him all my master's store,
> Who in his wrath did so loud upbraid
> And brought before the judge this Convict Maid.
>
> *The Convict Maid*

THE convict maid in the street ballad stole to keep her lover in luxury. That is her story. No doubt, the particular reasons why each female transportee committed a crime, which was to lead her to the penal colonies, differ in detail. To explain fully and satisfactorily the reasons why nearly 300 Welsh women committed crimes one would need to know all the circumstances and every life history and we simply have no record of all this. However, obviously, there are common elements in the women's conditions and I propose to examine briefly a number of possible reasons for the committal of crimes by the convict women. The first two suggested causes were considered very important by contemporaries. They are Drink and Ignorance . . . both words so redolent of Victorian moralising—they were discussed endlessly in the nineteenth century. Thirdly, there was the issue of poverty. Contemporary opinion was strictly divided about the role of poverty as a cause of crime and some even saw the reverse as a cause. Linked to poverty is the question of unsatisfactory home backgrounds of some of the convict women, though this is not an issue which greatly concerned writers in the nineteenth century. Occasionally one gets a glimpse into the early home life of a convict girl and it is sometimes startling. Finally, it is relevant to consider if there were any special factors which impelled women, rather than men, to crime.

Contemporaries were in little doubt that one of the chief and most pernicious of the causes of crime was the Demon Drink. In order to convey accurately both the sentiments and the tone of the nineteenth-century philanthropists, moralists, criminologists and lawyers, I report them here largely in their own words. Chief Baron Kelly at the Carmarthenshire Spring Assizes of 1872, said:

> Excess in drinking is the besetting sin of the lower class, and, perhaps, I may go further and say, classes and persons above their station, are the present cause of at least two-thirds of the crime committed in this country.

In Denbighshire Sir W. Bovill at the Assizes in August of the same year stated:

> Drunkenness, according to my experience, is at the root of nine-tenths of the crime committed in this Country.

In reading the reports of a succession of chaplains at Cardiff gaol in the second half of the nineteenth century, the story is always the same. In 1873 J. Rowlands Jones listed the following factors as causes of crime, 'drunkenness, prostitution, vagrancy, professional thieves and persons inflicted with cleptomania.' In 1875 the same chaplain gave his personal view on the major causes of crime. 'My experience in the past year', he wrote, 'has confirmed [me] in the opinion which I had previously formed and expressed that drunkenness is the principal cause of crime in this country. During the protracted and disastrous strike which took place in South Wales last winter, the number of prisoners in this gaol fell off so perceptibly that one could come to no other conclusion then that high wages are ruinous to working people in their present condition.'

Employers were positively doing the country good and benefitting the working class by paying low wages and thereby saving working people from the evils of drink! The notorious 1847 *Report on the State of Education in Wales* paints a very black picture of life in the principality and we should be wary about accepting its findings uncritically. But the evidence of an excess of drinking that it presents cannot be wholly dismissed, though one would add there is no reason to think of Wales as particularly worse than the rest of Great Britain. The report does show how easily available drink was. The rector of Llanhilleth, Monmouthshire, gave the facts about his parish as follows:

> There are in this small parish eight public-houses, five of which have spirit licences. The frequency of these houses in a parish comparatively agricultural and thinly populated has often been to me a matter of no small surprise. The Pontypool bench of magistrates have more than once pointedly said [when cases from this parish were brought before them], that Llanhilleth gives them much trouble.

But, at least, that rector had the sense to turn the tables on the magistrates and accuse them of corruptly disposing of spirits' licences in exchange for political support. Similarly the incumbent at Trevethin, writing from Pontypool was aware of the dangers of drink. 'The bane of the manufacturing districts is the beer shops', he said. 'They ruin the morals of every neighbourhood. Drunkenness is the crying sin of our working class, and by the facility which beer-houses afford of inducing people to drink, multitudes are led astray.' He went on to explain that part of the reason for the excess of drunkenness was the lack of other less harmful amusements in South Wales:

> The mass of our population are slaves to intemperate habits, and consequently they have scarcely any taste for such pursuits as would tend to the improvement of their minds and morals. Often, for the want of public amusements (such as would afford real recreation for mind and body), they flock to the beer-shops for them. The great desideratum in our manufacturing districts seems, to my mind, to be the establishment of such recreation as would divert from such grovelling pursuits and pleasures as beer-shops afford.

In 1849 Jellinger C. Symons, a commissioner in the inquiry of 1847 and a keen criminologist, stated that drink was the most 'fearfully powerful' cause of crime. He wrote:

> Perhaps of all the proximate causes of crime none is more fearfully powerful than that of drink, and the facilities and temptations to it which the law permits, most disastrously for the morals and welfare of the people. No statistics are needed on this subject: every town swarms with beer-houses and public-houses, the majority of them being ill-conducted, and in towns some are the haunts of thieves, prostitutes and gamblers.

Contemporaries thought that drink had an even more pernicious role to play in female crime. George Laval Chesterton, who was Governor of the House of Correction at Cold Bath Fields for twenty-five years, stated in his *Revelations of Prison Life*, that once drink had hold of women it would draw them down inexorably. He wrote:

> Experience taught me the utter hopelessness of reform (especially in the female character), when once that accursed craving had assumed a chronic form. No earthly consideration would seem equal to arrest the mastery of that unappeasable vice. In its vortex, every moral and social obligation becomes alike engulfed. The comforts of home, the advantages of station, or the sanctity of kindred—even of maternal ties—prove insufficient barriers against

73

the inroads of that fatal thirst. It drowns all reflection, and plunges its willing votary into any excess of crime and dishonour for its own insatiate gratification.

Finally, the anonymous author of the paper Criminal Women, previously quoted in this work, did not ascribe to drink the dominant role that other authorities did. Yet she/he paints an interesting picture of just how common a habit drunkenness was among criminal women.

All, or nearly all, are drunkards. Old, middle-aged, and young, their habits require stimulants. Without dram-drinking they could hardly go through their career. One fact we have noticed with regard to this habit which may be worth the attention of philanthropists. The victims groan under it. An address on drunkenness invariably moves them to tears. They know well what the habit had done for them, and they know equally well that it is like a long and heavy chain around them, that it binds them fast; and that reason as they will when gin is not within reach, they will take the cup directly they can get it. Many a female hawker under 21 has confessed that she is 'muddled' every night—mostly drunk; and has excused herself by saying that standing about the streets in all weathers is such miserable work, that she finds it impossible to refuse the many offers she has in the course of the day 'to take a drop.' Others again excuse themselves by the dreadful craving which follows upon each indulgence. Excessive drinking, as is well known, destroys the taste for wholesome food, where it can be procured. 'More, more', is the drunkard's cry, and nothing but 'more' gives her a temporary satisfaction.

One could go on adding to the nineteenth-century statements linking crime and alcohol. But enough is enough. Clearly there was some association between the two. We don't know how many respectable women were reduced to the criminal class through drink or how many law abiding women, fuddled for the first time by alcohol, committed a crime. But certainly there is evidence of the problem of drink in connection with some of the female transportees. One Glamorgan woman was described in Tasmanian records, which refer to her on arrival, as a 'dissolute drunkard'. In the same set of records, which also chart the women's progress in the colony, there are many references to punishments inflicted on women for drunk and disorderly behaviour. For example, Mary Davies, a London woman, transported by a court in Carmarthen, received fourteen days' imprisonment in Tasmania for drunkenness. There are many similar cases. The difficulty is, however, to know how many of the convicts were drinkers *before* they were sent

74

to Australia. I do not doubt that many later became so as a consequence of the brutalising system.

It does seem likely that there was a connection between drink and crime, but drink is an inadequate explanation for crime and is merely symptomatic of a more serious malaise in society. Strong drink offered the quickest road out of Manchester, as the saying goes. It was also the shortest route out of Cardiff, Swansea, Merthyr or anywhere else. One has to bear in mind the very difficult living conditions especially in industrialised South Wales, where many convict women had been convicted, to understand the urgency of some people to escape reality.

Ignorance—the appalling lack of education of the working classes—ranked a close second to drink as a cause of crime in the eyes of many nineteenth-century moralists. Mary Carpenter, the Bristol woman, who was the leading advocate of reform schools (instead of prisons) for children, saw ignorance as the chief cause of crime. In her book, *Reformatory Schools for the Children of the Perishing and Dangerous Classes and for Juvenile Offenders*, she tells horrific tales of infants fending for themselves on city streets and turning inevitably to crime. She saw the basic solution to this many sided problem in education. She concentrated on helping children, i.e. 'the infant population', which she described as springing up 'rank and noxious in a hot bed of vice.' She made a distinction between the perishing and the dangerous classes as follows:

> That part of the community which we are to consider, consists of those who have not yet fallen into actual crime, but who are almost certain from their ignorance, destitution, and the circumstances in which they are growing up, to do so, if a helping hand be not extended to raise them, — these form the perishing classes: — and of those who have already received the prison brand, or, if the mark has not been yet visibly set upon them, are notoriously living by plunder, — who unblushingly acknowledge that they can gain more for the support of themselves and their parents by stealing than by working, — whose hand is against every man, for they know not that any man is their brother; — these form the dangerous classes.

Mary Carpenter believed that education was the most immediate way of helping all these people and quite a lot of authorities agreed with her, or at least pontificated, even if they did nothing. In the House of Lords for example Lord Cockburn expressed the conviction, 'I am confident that this education must materially diminish crime . . . it is our great hope.'

But there was not unanimity on the links between crime and ignorance. Some people believed that education would make criminals more efficient and that the acquisition of literary skills would open up new avenues of crime, for example, forgery and embezzlement. As Jellinger C. Symons bewailed, what passed for education in England and Wales would instead of checking crime, largely increase it, 'by giving mental power to moral evil.' Symons argued that it was not among the totally illiterate that crime was increasing but among those who had some smattering of education. Being able to read stirring and corrupting literature, such as cheap pamphlets on Dick Turpin or that other well known criminal, Jack Shephard, was positively damaging. Perhaps there is something in what one witness had to say before a Select Committee on Police in 1828:

> I confess I think the *over education* (!) of the lower class of the people has done harm. I do not mean to say that it is not desirable that children should be educated, but if they are to be educated and afterward have no employment, you have merely given them the expertness to become thieves.

Actually it is quite difficult to assess the contribution of a lack of any education to crime. We know that there was only a limited amount of education available to the Welsh working classes and that if we believe only a tenth of the 1847 report we see that the standards were generally quite low. Moreover, there is plenty of evidence to show the ignorance of prisoners. In the late 1840s the chaplain at Brecon Gaol, though reporting that most prisoners there could read and write imperfectly, showed how shallow their knowledge was. Six out of every ten prisoners did not know the name of the father of Jesus Christ and five out of ten did not know the Queen's name. Prisoners were officially classified into groups according to educational attainment. They were:

i.e.	N	. . .	neither read nor write
	Imp	. . .	read and write imperfectly
	Well	. . .	read and write well
	Sup	. . .	superior education

Needless to say I have come across no female convict in Wales designated as 'sup'.

If we confined our attention specifically to female prisoners the picture is certainly one of uneducated women. The writer in the *Cornhill Magazine* says they are grossly ignorant and when asking a woman if she knew who the Saviour was received the reply, 'I beg your pardon; I am not a larned woman.' Turning to the Welsh convict women in particular, there is more precise evidence extant on their education. However, it is limited and it would be rash to generalise from it. Between 1830 and 1852, forty-two women sentenced by courts in Glamorgan sailed to Tasmania; of these forty-two, the educational attainment of twenty-five is known. A slightly different educational classification system was used and its findings are:

Read and Write	...	4
Read	...	17
No Education	...	4

There is no knowing what meagre attainment lies behind the description 'able to read.' Moreover, it should be noted that these figures come from the later part of the transportation era and probably show a higher level than they would have done for the earlier part of the period.

Hardly any attempts were made to educate prisoners in Wales, as far as I know. By the 1870s Cardiff gaol had no professional teacher. In some large London prisons, however, some provisions were made to educate prisoners. Millbank, which many Welsh convict women passed through en route to Australia, did attempt to educate its charges. The matron records that there was no enthusiasm for the reading and writing lessons, in fact less so than for their normal prison work. Nevertheless, at Millbank the staff ventured briefly to teach arithmetic. The experiment failed as the matron noted and as the following scene indicates:

> At one period an attempt was made to teach the elementary rules of arithmetic, a variation which unfortunately proved a signal failure. It was the last feather on the camel's back, and the women would have nothing to do with such arduous mental exertion. To do them justice they made the attempt; but the extraordinary answers that were returned to questions the most simple, and the shouts of laughter from the women at the desks at the blunders of those who had found courage to respond, were subversive of good order, often of good temper. A scene like the subjoined was of common occurrence:
> 'Attention, please, twice two?'
> 'Four' would be responded pretty generally.
> 'Twice three?'
> Affairs would be growing difficult, and out of twenty-five women six or seven would venture to reply, 'Six'.
> 'Twice four?'
> Dead silence to be suddenly broken by one voice crying out, 'Nine', at which there would be a roar of laughter from the rest of the class.
> 'What are you laughing at, stupids?' I have heard a woman passionately exclaim; 'I'll fetch one of you a hit of the mouth in a minute, if you don't stop grinning.'

> 'Jackson, I shall report you', remonstrates the matron on the watch.
> 'I ain't come here to be laughed at, miss, I can tell you!'
> Jackson will probably subside, if the matron be a woman of tact and well acquainted with the humours of the prisoners.

Another distinguished feature of Millbank was its library, but the range of books it contained shows how hopelessly out of touch with the women the authorities were and how ill-designed these works were to encourage a person to read. They were mainly religious works and volumes on the history of Carthage, Greece and Rome.

Ignorance—though thought of by many contemporaries as a cause of crime—would be seen by most nowadays as just one aspect of a wider problem. The chronic condition of much of the working class in nineteenth-century Britain stemmed from poverty and a very unequal distribution of wealth. Education was merely one of the things money could buy and probably not one which many people would have put very high on their list of priorities. Food, a home and warmth were far more important for people to acquire and it is to the absence of these basic necessities of life that we must next look.

There was contemporary disagreement too as to the role of poverty as a cause of crime. A Royal Commission of 1839 on the Constabulary Force utterly dismissed poverty as a cause of crime. Crime it said was caused by the temptations of the high-life and not by poverty.

> We have investigated the origin of the great mass of crime committed for the sake of property, and we find the whole ascribable to one common cause, namely, the temptations of the profit of a career of depredation, as compared with the profits of honest and even well paid industry . . . The notion that any considerable proportion of the crimes against property are caused by blameless poverty or destitution we find disproved at every step.

Others saw the great need of the poor in both urban and rural areas as inextricably bound up with crime. Some nineteenth-century writers examined in detail the correlation between high prices and the crime rate and clearly demonstrated the link between the two. It could easily be argued that crime should be regarded as social protest. Not surprisingly, the crime rate rose in the bad years following the end of the Napoleonic wars in 1815 and in the difficult times of the 1830s and 1840s, which in Wales were marked by disturbances at Merthyr, by the activities of the Chartists and by the Rebecca riots. The precise correlation between crime and prices is a complex issue and often involves specific local factors which do not concern us here. Yet it is essential to realise that poverty formed the background to many of the crimes committed by the Welsh female transportees.

The proof of the link between hardship and the crimes of the female transportees is quite obvious. The nature of the great majority of crimes illustrated this. Their crimes were very small scale. The objects they stole were worn clothing, bedding or food. Who would indulge in such petty theft, given the dreadful punishment they risked? There is plenty of evidence to show that transportation was a feared punishment. Who, unless quite desperate, would risk this sentence for a cheese or a pair of shoes? One cannot compare the thefts committed by these women with those of shoplifting by quite wealthy women today. The latter only risk a fine, which they can easily pay.

I have found only two statements from transportees themselves giving their own motives for crime. Charlotte Davies in Caernarvonshire tried to sell an apron she had stolen, because she was 'just famished with hunger', Jane Griffiths, of the same county, was selling off the goods she had stolen because, she said, 'I am in want of meat.'

Some contemporaries, even some of those in authority in Australia, were inclined to believe these women and men. Sir George Arthur affirmed before the 1837 Select Committee on Transportation, 'I think that many of those who have been sent out here have been driven to commit the offence through want.'

Poverty was obviously detrimental to a secure family life and it may well have been the case that some of the convict women came from what would now be considered very difficult backgrounds. Not surprisingly, there is very little information on the intimacies of the home life of the transportees but there are a few glimpses. Ellen Reece, who was born 'somewhere in Wales' and grew up there, while awaiting transportation, after being sentenced in Salford, was required to complete a questionnaire for the Royal Commission of the Constabulary force. Some of her answers range back over her earlier life, though she was only 24 at the time of responding:

> *What has been your calling or occupation*? Domestic Servant for six months at about 16 years of age.
> *Are your Parents living? If not, what was your age when they or either of them died?* Mother is living. Father died when she was 13.
> *If either Father or Mother be dead, has the survivor married again? If so, how long ago?* Mother still a Widow—out of 18 children only Ellen and two older alive. Sister 29—Brother 28 both respectable, most died young.
> *Are you illegitimate? or a foundling?* Legitimate.
> *Where were you brought up? At the house of your Parents or at that of any other relation or friend? Or in the workhouse. Or in*

the streets, being left without care and control? Was brought up by Parents 'till 14.

Of what calling were your Parents? Did they, or either of them, continue long in any service? Father was a Slap-dasher, Mother kept house—Father worked for himself.

Of what character was your Father? Was he honest, industrious and sober? Was honest and industrious, but fond of drink.

Of what character was your Mother? Was she honest, virtuous, industrious, and sober? Mother was all these.

Did your Parents regularly attend a place of worship, and require you to accompany them? Yes, the Welch Independents. They always saw her to School every Sunday—Mr. Roby's and Independent Sunday School.

What care was taken of you by your Parents? Did you ever run away from them? What induced you to so? Were you punished for doing so and in what way? The greatest care as could be took of a child. First ran away from home six months after Father's death then between 13 and 14, took some of her clothes and pawned them at a neighbours, said her Mother wanted to make rent up. Got 11s. and went away without any object, met a Girl who had stolen some Clothes who asked her to go with her to pawn them, she got a good deal and she took Reece to a cellar in Shudehill where there were about nine young Girls younger than herself, not for prostitution but to watch people out of their houses and commit thefts—no men went there. Mother found her after three days, took her home, beat her with a rod for a quarter of an hour . . .

Did the occupation of either of your Parents necessarily take them from home? Mother sold Eggs and took in Lodgers.

What was the immediate cause of your first offence? Whether to procure any particular gratification, and of what kind? From sudden temptation, or opportunity; if so, of what kind? Or from distress; whether from imprudence of other misconducts? About two days before she went her mother boxed her, and she said to herself, 'She was old enough to take care of herself without being beat.' Kept getting her things by degrees and then went off. Did not know whether to turn back or not—heart filled.

Ellen Reece reacted against her mother, but at least her mother seemed caring. Eliza Williams, a red-haired farm servant in Breconshire, had a difficult home life. There is no mention of a mother but her father was a drover and often away. He took 'little or no account of her' and she got in with very bad company. She was transported in 1832 for stealing clothes. One wonders about some of the families of the female transportees on finding more than one transportee coming from the same family. The two sisters, Elizabeth and Catherine Jones, aged 17 and 34 respectively, were tried on the same day in Caernarvonshire and transported on the same ship, the *Sovereign*, in 1827. Sarah Smart from Monmouthshire told the authorities her sister had already been transported and one of Mary Ann Powhill's sisters had been transported ten years' earlier. Many of the women came from very large families—as was normal in those days. The family of one Glamorgan woman presents an interesting mixture: Jane Evans was transported and had been two years on the town, whereas her brother, John, had become a clergyman in Staffordshire.

The causes of crime already noted were all, of course, common to both men and women. There are, however, a few additional factors which ought to be taken into consideration when discussing why women committed crimes.

Opportunities for working class men and women were very limited, but there were even more restraints on the lives of working class women than on those of the men. Many well paid or skilled jobs were not open to them and even when women did the same jobs as men they were paid far less—normally about half. This inability to command a good wage is very important here because the majority of the convict women were single and had to support themselves, by their own labours. Many of them entered domestic service. The census of 1851 shows that domestic service was by far the largest single type of employment of women and that in that year nearly one million women were 'in service'. At that date servants were still largely country girls who came to the towns for work. This was the pattern in Wales. With little work available in small rural communities, the adolescent daughter of a family would move off to employment in a town in order to relieve the family of the burden of keeping her. In service she would be provided with board and lodgings in addition to a wage. Wages varied from household to household. Large establishments with many servants paid best, but there were not many of these in Wales. The country girl would very likely enter the house of a lower middle class family, where she was often the solitary maid-of-all-work or perhaps one of two young girls kept there. Many of the convicts called themselves kitchen-maids or house-servants. The recommended wage for a kitchen-maid suggested in *The Complete Servant* published in London in 1825, was £14 per annum and that for a dairy-maid on a large country estate was £8. But sixty years later a good general servant in South Wales could hope to receive £12 a year. The quality of board varied too. It might be quite good in a large house, but it might have meant little more than scraps in a one-servant house. Hours were very long, often from 5.00 a.m to 10.00 p.m. The work was heavy and severe . . . carrying coals and water, emptying baths, moving solid wooden furniture. Women who spent their lives in service rarely married and many honest ones ended up in the workhouse. Prince Albert himself was very concerned at the large numbers of old servants who ended their days as workhouse paupers.

Hard work, low wages in small households and strict discipline from employers made domestic service an unattractive proposition. Young working class girls envied the better money, companionship and freedom of those free spirits, the factory girls. But there was hardly any factory work for them in Wales and, beyond domestic service, there really was no choice for most girls.

Another fairly large group of Welsh convict women remained in the countryside and were employed as farm servants. Some were outdoor workers and this was considered far less respectable than being a servant indoors. Contemporaries thought women were coarsened by this work not only because of the heavy manual labour involved but also because the field workers worked in mixed groups and men and women openly fraternised! Farm workers received a wage and usually no board. It was also seasonal work. They were hired when required and laid off when not. The indoor farm girls and dairy-maids considered themselves superior to the outdoor servants in husbandry. The dairy-maid could be reasonably well off: she often received board as well as a wage and she possessed very marketable skills.

Many of the Welsh convict women had children to support. Some of these mothers were widows, but most were single women. The position was enormously difficult. They had to take on the role of the bread winner, but they could not command a man's wages. Given these difficulties, some turned to prostitution, others to crime and some to both.

We have to remember that these women lived against a background of hypocrisy and Victorian moralising. A pregnancy would literally *ruin* a single woman. Her descent from the ranks of the respectable could be rapid and irrevocable. It would be very interesting to find out how different communities in eighteenth and nineteenth-century Wales reacted to this event, as there may well have been a wide variety of responses. The reaction of righteous horror was, however, quite a widespread one and Mrs. Robinson, matron of Millbank, tells a melodramatic but very sad little tale about one Welsh girl, whom she names Jane Ellis for secrecy's sake. Ellis lived in a little village 'nestling among the Welsh mountains.' Her father was a comfortably off small holder and a Methodist. One day an Englishman on a walking tour paused a few days at the village inn and the tall, graceful, warmhearted Welsh girl took his fancy and he seduced her. He promised to marry her and she waited anxiously for him to return. Of course, he never did. She was thrown out of her home by her parents and then out of the village by the others. She turned to the streets to keep herself and her baby and then

Millbank penitentiary: entrance to pentagon

she spiralled downwards, via petty larceny, to Millbank penitentiary. The awful drama of Mrs. Robinson's tale lies in the way her story ended. Ellis, who was by now a very refractory prisoner and an anti-social woman, was sitting at her cell door one day when who should pass but a pious prison visitor. It was the self same villain who had occasioned her fall! This is a true story and Mrs. Robinson believed it. Without the dramatic ending of the prison encounter, similar tales may well have been enacted many times over.

Finally, the more one examines the causes of crime the more the question in one's mind changes from 'Why did people commit crime?' to 'Why did more people not commit crimes, given the awful circumstances?' The answer to the new question, however, is largely answered by a consideration of the dreadful punishments administered to those who were found guilty of crime. To see just what a deterrent legal punishments could be we need to look at transportation in operation.

The inner gate at Millbank

Chapter 6

THE VOYAGES

> There's the Captain as is our Commander
> There's the bosun and all the ships crew,
> There's the first and second class passengers,
> Knows what we poor convicts go through.
>
> *Botany Bay*

ONCE sentence of transportation had been passed, the convicted woman would be returned to the gaol to await conveyance to a port of departure. The delay which took place before she was removed to one of the major ports could be quite considerable, especially in the early years of the transportation system. Sarah Richards, for example, a woman transported by a Glamorgan court, was tried in March 1796 but her ship did not sail until June 1801. Mary Lewis, who had been tried at Merioneth Court of Great Sessions in 1793, was aboard the same vessel!

The conditions in the prisons in which the women languished before sailing were usually quite appalling. Often these gaols were verminous hovels, where disease thrived: many had no water supply or sewers and bedding meant a pile of rags on a bare damp floor. First-time offenders were thrown in with dissolute and hardened old criminals and in the eighteenth century there was rarely any segregation between the male and female prisoners. In the 1770s John Howard toured the gaols of England and Wales and was horrified by what he saw. He reports that, in his opinion, more prisoners died of 'gaol fever' (typhoid) than were put to death by all the public executions in the kingdom. Prisoners were laden with 'heavy irons which make their walking and even lying down to sleep difficult and painful', unless, of course, they could afford to bribe the gaoler to spare them from the irons. Howard provides us with alarming descriptions of many Welsh gaols. He describes the county Bridewell at Cowbridge, Glamorgan, as housing prisoners mainly in two rooms each 15 feet square. These rooms were in fact well ventilated, not to say cold, but nevertheless the gaol-keeper told Howard that many had died there of the gaol fever and that he and his daughter had both been struck down by the sickness. The prison was not secure and it provided no employment for its inmates. Of the old gaol at Haverfordwest, Howard wrote that the two lowest rooms were damp dungeons in which one prisoner had lost first the 'use of his limbs and then his life.' The higher rooms were very dirty and offensive and there was no sanitation. However, a new provision for prisoners was being made in Pembrokeshire. In Merionethshire in the 1780s prisoners at the Clifton gaol were driven to petition the court of Quarter Sessions because their water supply was full of maggots and filth.

In fact, it is very difficult to understand how eighteenth-century prisons functioned. Prisoners were expected to pay fees on entering and leaving the gaol and in many cases to buy their own food. Many certainly were at near starvation level and when one looks at the gaoler's provision lists one sees how abysmal the diet was. In 1798 Thomas Morgan, gaoler in Cardiff, presented a bill for provisions which consisted mainly of sheep's heads, 'beef's heads', assorted bones and bread.

A perusal of old gaol records sometimes enables one to spot a transportee awaiting transferral to the ships. At Brecon gaol a certain Catherine Connick, aged 29 at the time of conviction and found guilty of stealing from the person, was awaiting transportation for life. Throughout the year 1832 there are constant references to her in the gaoler's accounts because she was in very poor health. In the spring she was served with extra oatmeal at a cost of one shilling and fourpence to the county. By the summer she was not eating solids and was being fed on gruel. The gaoler's account reads, '14 basons of gruel for C. Connick from June 26 to July 10th by order of the surgeon', and again '32 basons at 2½d. . . . 6s. 8d.' She also had a pair of stockings provided for her to wear in gaol at a cost of one shilling and a penny. But Catherine Connick never did sail off to Australia and it would seem reasonable to presume that she died.

For those who actually did sail the next step was conveyance either to a central prison in London, where transportees from all over Britain were collected together, or directly to the convict ships. The sheriff of the county of committal would receive an order from the central government authorising the conveyance of a convict to the ship. The following letter shows such an order from Whitehall to transfer a Caernarvonshire woman to Woolwich.

Whitehall, 15 June, 1825

Sir,

In pursuance of an Act passed in the Fifth Year of the Reign of His present Majesty, intituled 'An Act for the Transportation of Offenders', from Great Britain . . . I do hereby authorise and direct you to cause the . . . . . . Eleanor Williams . . . . Female Convicts named in the Margin, now under Sentence of Transportation in the Gaol at Carnarvon, to be removed with all convenient Speed after the Receipt of this Order, on board the Ship Midas lying at Woolwich, and there delivered to the Contractor or Master of the said Ship, if the said Convicts, upon being examined by an experienced Surgeon or Apothecary, shall be found free from any putrid or infectious Distemper, and fit to be removed from the Gaol. The Contractor or Master will give you a Receipt for your Discharge. You will at the same time deliver to him a Certificate specifying concisely the Description of each Prisoner's Crime, her Age, whether married or unmarried, her Trade or Profession and an Account of her Behaviour in Prison before and after her Trial, and the Gaoler's Observations on her Temper and Disposition, and such information concerning her Connexions and former Course of Life, as may have come to the Gaoler's Knowledge. You will also transmit to this Office a true Copy, attested by you or by the Gaoler having the Custody of the said Convicts, of the Caption, and Order of the Court by which each of the said Offenders was sentenced or ordered for Transportation.

The Convicts must be cleanly and properly clothed, and each of them provided with the Articles of Wearing Apparel as undermentioned. Children whose Ages do not exceed, if Boys 6 Years, and Girls 10 Years, will be allowed to accompany their Mothers, but if either of such Convicts should have a Child at the Breast, she must not be removed on board the said Ship.

> I am,
> Sir,
> Your most obedient,
> humble Servant,
>
> Norbur

Convicts were fettered in irons for the journey to London or the ship. An escort accompanied them. The modes of travel were somewhat varied, as the expenses of a male convict taken from Cardiff to London en route for Africa show. Expenses included chaise hire, boat hire, coach from Bristol to London, turnpike tolls, overnight expenses at a London inn and the hire of a small boat to take him to the transport vessel. The accounts also survive for the journey of another male convict from Merionethshire to Portsmouth. He and his escort travelled on horseback to Shrewsbury and then by stage coach to London. Travel by stage coach should not conjure up a cosy picture since convicts travelled on the outside and in fetters. The wearing of irons by the convict may well have been an unnecessary precaution since a few months in a Welsh gaol was probably sufficiently debilitating to stop an escaper getting far. However, there are instances not only of individual convicts in shackles but of groups of convicts being chained together. In 1823 eleven women travelled from Lancaster to London with iron hoops around their arms and legs and they could not 'get up or down from the coach without the whole being dragged together.' Of course, there was an alternative means of transport to the ports. From some Welsh counties it was cheaper to despatch convicts by sea. Several Caernarvonshire and Merionethshire convicts travelled in this way.

Female convicts from all over Britain were usually gathered together at a major London prison before being escorted to the dockside. At first, and for many years, Newgate was the collecting point. This prison was a true chamber of horrors and Elizabeth Fry, the Quaker reformer, felt as though she was 'going into a den of wild beasts', and she reflects, 'quite shuddering' when the door closed upon her and she was 'locked in with a herd of novel and desperate companions.' Women, men, children, old offenders and first timers and indeed innocent people, awaiting trial, were confined together at Newgate. With no uniform provided, many wore rags. Again Elizabeth Fry describes the goings on there, 'the begging, swearing, gaming, fighting, singing, dancing, dressing up in men's clothes: scenes too bad to be described.' In later years the great penitentiary at Millbank on the Thames replaced Newgate as a clearing house for female transportees. Conditions there were very different from Newgate, with its filth and laxity. Millbank aimed at cleanliness and efficiency and was in its way just as soul destroying as Newgate had ever been. We know a great deal about conditions at Millbank from the matron's memoirs. She describes the enrolment of each new inmate there in these words:

> A registry of name, a shortening of hair, a tepid bath, a change in the dress in which they are received to the brown serge, blue check apron, a muslin cap of prison uniform, the key turned upon the cell . . .

It is interesting that she records that the first new rule to which the prisoner must submit, and a trial which they found hardest to bear, was having their hair cut short. It is worth pausing over this tiny detail to see the depersonalising process to which the convict women were subjected. Mrs. Robinson recounted:

> With a woman new to the rules, a comer who has not sat in that room before, with the scissors of Atropos snipping round her

Millbank: women prisoners at exercise

head, it is seldom performed without a remonstrance. Women whose hearts have not quailed, perhaps, at the murder of their infants, of the poisoning of their husbands, clasp their hands in horror at this sacrifice of their natural adornment—weep, beg, pray, occasionally assume a defiant attitude and resist to the last, and are finally only overcome by force. It is one of the most painful tasks of the prison, this hair-cutting operation—moreover, it is, in my opinion, at least, a test of character.

And again she notes the pathetic story of an old prisoner and her touching faith in the British law on matrimony:

The greatest trouble in my experience of prison life was with an old woman of sixty years of age, and with about the same number of grey hairs to her head. She was an old prison-bird—had spent two-thirds of her life in prison, and was as vain of her personal appearance as any girl of seventeen.

89

'No, Miss B.,' she said to the operator, after catching sight of the scissors, and drawing herself up with the haughtiness of a duchess—'not this time, if you please, Miss B. It can't be done.' But Miss B. replied it could be done, and was absolutely necessary to be done before the prisoner left the room.

'Things have altered a little, Miss B., since I saw you last, I can assure you. You've no power to touch a hair of my head, mum.'

'How's that?'

'If you please, mum, I'm married', and the old woman regarded the matron with undisguised triumph.

'And what's that to do with it?—sit down—you really must sit down.'

'What's that to do with it!' shrieked the old woman, indignantly; 'Why, it's my husband's hair now, and you daren't touch it, according to law. It belongs to my husband, not to me, and you've no right to touch it. Lord bless you, the Queen of England daren't lay a finger on it now!'

Millbank, however, was far from satisfactory as a clearing house. It turned out to be a very unhealthy place and in 1849 inspectors reported that the conduct of women transferred to the ships from local prisons was far better than that of those from Millbank.

The next leg of the convict woman's journey was to the port. As regards the journey from Newgate, Elizabeth Fry was personally responsible for a great improvement. The old practice was for the women to be conveyed in irons and upon open waggons to the docks. But in 1818 Elizabeth Fry had this changed. Her daughter relates:

It was a practice among the female transports to riot previous to their departure from Newgate, breaking windows, furniture or whatever came within their reach. They were generally conveyed from the prison to the waterside in open wagons, went off amidst assembled crowds and were noisy and disorderly on the roads and in the boats. Mrs. Fry prevailed upon the governor to consent to their being moved in hackney coaches. She promised the women that if they were quiet and orderly that she and other ladies would accompany them to Deptford and see them on board: accordingly when the time came no disturbance took place: the women in hackney coaches with turnkeys in attendance formed a procession which was closed by her carriage and the women behaved well upon the road.

That first convict ship to which Elizabeth Fry accompanied the transportees was the *Maria*. On board it were three Welsh women who would almost certainly have met her, as she took personal responsibility for

Millbank: the prison graveyard

organising them into groups of companions for the journey. These Welsh women were Mary Williams and Mary Roberts of Caernarvonshire, and Margaret Watkins of Monmouthshire.

As for the journey in later years from Millbank to the 'Bay ships' as they were commonly called, it was a very short land trip. Millbank was actually on the Thames and the convicts were embarked just outside. Another nineteenth-century writer with an intimate knowledge of Millbank, Major A. Griffiths, states that convicts were never informed until the night before embarkation that the hour of departure had come. Then they were awakened at 3.00 a.m., their names checked, they were shackled and placed in gangs of ten. In the grey light of dawn they filed across the deserted roadway, down the steps and into a steam tug (in the 1840s) which conveyed them to a transport vessel moored at the Nore. When the tide was low the problem of embarking them on to the steam tug was solved by an old bargee named Collins. This old Collins, who made a living fishing dead bodies out of the Thames, ran his barges aground and thereby formed a bridge between the river bank and the steam tug. In the company of the deputy governor of the prison and the warders, the convicts passed down to Gravesend and on to the Nore, where they saw the convict vessel with the Blue Peter flying.

91

The First Fleet

As to the actual sea journeys to Australia, the early voyages of the eighteenth century have commanded most attention. The voyages of the First and Second Fleets have been carefully studied and quite a lot is known about them. The First Fleet stands out simply because it was the first and because, in some ways, it was a remarkably successful enterprise. The Second Fleet, on the other hand, has gained a reputation for less impressive reasons. It was an appallingly badly organised expedition and it has won notoriety for its infamously vile conditions on board. Both fleets deserve a brief examination here as women from Wales sailed with both.

In 1787 the First Fleet under the able command of Governor Arthur Philip, sailed for New South Wales, where Philip was to take up the appointment of the first governorship. It was a very large undertaking. A voyage of over 15,000 miles and over eight months at sea lay before them. The fleet consisted of eleven vessels, six of which carried convicts. The size of the vessels was horrifyingly small by modern standards. The longest convict ship was only 114 feet in length and 31 feet in breadth at the widest part. Others were just over a 100 feet long and 29 feet wide. For the most part they were three masted and square rigged vessels. On these eleven ships, 1,480 people sailed and more than half of that number were convicts. There were 568 male and 191 female convicts on board at the time of sailing. (Sixteen men and one woman had died from an epidemic before the fleet put out). Distribution of the convicts aboard the vessels was as follows:

	Convicts	
Vessel	Male	Female
Alexander	195	—
Charlotte	88	20
Friendship	76	21
Lady Penrhyn	—	101
Prince of Wales	1	49
Scarborough	208	—

In addition to the convicts and crew, the fleet carried provisions, sheep, hogs and goats.

Of the female convicts on the First Fleet only two came from Wales. They were 19-year-old Mary Watkins of St. Andrews, Glamorgan: she had stolen clothing and had originally been sentenced to transportation to Africa. She was aboard the *Friendship*. The other woman, Frances Williams, had been tried at Mold, Flintshire, four years earlier for housebreaking. Her sentence was 'that she be taken to a place of Execution and hanged by the neck until she be dead', but she was subsequently pardoned on condition that she was transported beyond the sea for seven years. She was embarked on to the transport, *The Prince of Wales*.

The initial preparations of the British government for the voyage of the First Fleet were grossly inadequate and Governor Philip had constantly to badger the authorities for improvements. He was aghast at the sight of the female convicts as they boarded the vessels. Many were ill and suffering from venereal disease and other maladies. They were half-naked and in tatters and Governor Philip accused the government of 'infamy', as he demanded clothing for the wretched women. But the women had a long wait for their garments and, when they did arrive, they were of such poor quality that they fell to pieces within weeks. When this happened, the women were compelled to wear sacking.

The prison quarters were below decks. They were infested with rats, cockroaches and bugs. A young officer, on the First Fleet, records that he spent the whole of one July Sunday morning in his cramped sleeping quarters killing over 100 bugs with oil and tar and, it must be realised, that his quarters would have been far more comfortable than the convict prison. Attempts were made to purify the air by frequent explosions of gunpowder, lighting fires between decks and a liberal use of that admirable antiseptic oil of tar. Ventilation was always a problem in these vessels and the women suffered more than the men from foul air.

Aboard the convict ship *Success*, between decks looking for'ard
Radio Times Hulton Picture Library

At night the hatches were battened down over the women's prison in order to prevent men—crew or possibly male convicts—from reaching the women. The prisoners, both female and male, were in irons for some time. Many convicts had actually been put aboard the vessels two months before sailing, and their heavy irons were not struck off until, in this instance, they had been out at sea a week. By that time, according to one authority, the convicts were too dispirited and dejected from sea sickness to be much trouble.

The weather added to the discomfort of all aboard. The convict ships rolled and pitched and shipped a great deal of water. The swell rushed into the *Friendship*, pouring in between decks and washing the marines and the convict women out of their beds. Lieutenant Clark, aboard that vessel, records that by December it was very cold with snow and hail falling. In this bitter weather he wore two pairs of stockings and an extra flannel waistcoat and he was also obliged to keep his great coat on all the time. The convict women were wearing sacking by this time and

Painting by Lieut. William Bradley showing the First Fleet entering
Botany Bay, 1788
Australian Information Service, London

had one regulation blanket each. Cold and heavy seas made life difficult on the *Charlotte, Lady Penrhyn* and the *Prince of Wales* too. The surgeon aboard the *Lady Penrhyn* records that during a fierce storm in January:

> The convict women were so terrified that most of them were on their knees at prayers, and in less than one hour after it had abated they were uttering the most horrid oaths and imprecations that could proceed out of the mouths of such abandoned prostitutes as they are.

Food supplies, however, seem to have been quite good, thanks again to Philip. At the Cape, i.e. Cape Town, where the Fleet anchored, Philip purchased soft bread (a welcome change from sea biscuit), fresh vegetables and meat. He also bought live stock and the women convicts from the *Friendship*, including young Mary Watkins, were removed to the *Lady Penrhyn*, the *Charlotte* and the *Prince of Wales* in order to

95

make room for sheep. Lieut. Clark, aboard the *Friendship* remarked sneeringly:

> I am very glad of it, for they were great trouble and much more so than the men.

He expressed the hope of the sheep:

> We will find them much more agreeable shipmates than the women.

But the poor sheep were not very well looked after either and many died through storms or lack of fodder.

As to the women, there is evidence that some of them caused trouble aboard the vessels of the First Fleet. A handful of women on the *Friendship* were chiefly responsible. Four of them were punished for fighting. The incident occurred on the day before the Fleet left Teneriffe where it had put in. These women were punished by being put in irons for ten days. This was a severe punishment in view of the heat. A little later, a few of the same gang got into further trouble. It was discovered that some seamen had broken through the bulkhead into the women's prison and taken women back to their quarters with them. On discovery of the incident, the sailors were flogged and the women put in irons. Although, on this same vessel a woman who was abusive to the Captain was also flogged, tied to the mast and whipped with the cat in the fine old naval tradition. As that most unpleasant character, Lieut. Clark, remarked with relish, he was pleased that:

> the corporal did not play with her but laid it home.

Yet another woman who maligned the surgeon—a purely verbal attack—was bound and gagged. Aboard the *Lady Penrhyn* other punishments were administered to the women for fighting, bad language and thieving. These included the use of thumb screws, iron fetters on the wrists, flogging with the cat-of-nine-tails and the hated shaving-off of their hair.

Many of the details of life aboard the First Fleet are indeed horrific but at least the fleet enjoyed the services of conscientious surgeons and its death rate was remarkably low. Of the 568 men and 191 women who actually sailed only twenty men and three women died on the passage. The precautions taken to purify the air and Philip's insistence on anti-scurbotics made the voyage a singularly healthy one. As Surgeon Bowes of the *Lady Penrhyn* remarked:

> It is pretty extraordinary how very healthy the convicts on board this ship in particular and the Fleet in general have been during so long a passage and where there was a necessity of stowing them so thick together.

View of Botany Bay showing some First Fleet ships.
Painting by R. Cleveley

Australian Information Service, London

Two vessels sailed between the departure of the First and Second Fleets. They were the *Lady Juliana*, carrying female convicts and the *Guardian* carrying men.

The *Lady Juliana* was chartered by the British government to carry convicts to Australia and thereafter she was chartered by the East India Company to sail on to China and bring back tea. The naval agent on board, Thomas Edgar, had sailed with Captain Cook on his voyage of discovery to the southern continent and has won the reputation of being a kind and humanitarian gentleman. A mariner on board, John Nicol, notes that although Edgar would have been well within his rights to dispose of the women convicts' old clothing when they came aboard, he had it stowed in the hold on the grounds that they would be 'useful to the poor creatures when they arrived at Port Jackson.' Perhaps there were a few other generous spirits like Edgar or how else can one explain tales of the women landing in feathers, furs and other finery. A competent medical officer was also on board. The voyage was a long one for the 226 women since it took over ten months for the *Lady Juliana* to reach New South Wales. There were troubled incidents en route for many of these women were hardened London prostitutes but there were sad cases too and John Nicol tells the story of a little Scots girl, whom he says he could never get out of his mind:

> 'The young Scottish girl, I have never yet got out of my mind', declares Nicol. 'She was young and beautiful, even in the convict dress, but pale as death and her eyes red with weeping. She never spoke to any of the women or came on deck. She was constantly seen sitting in the same corner from morning till night; even the time of meals roused her not . . . At length she sunk into the grave of no disease but a broken heart.'

Nicol paints an interesting and lively picture of life on the long voyage of the *Lady Juliana*. Drink flowed freely on the ship and she has been described as a floating brothel. As Nicol said, 'When we were fairly out at sea every man on board took a wife from among the convicts, *they nothing loathe*.' We only have Nicol's word that the women were willing. Maybe some were but it may have made little difference if they were willing or not.

The *Guardian* may be mentioned here. She was the first convict ship to be wrecked. She struck an iceberg in fog 1,300 miles out from the Cape.

The voyage of the Second Fleet is a true marine horror story. The fleet was composed of only three vessels and carried male and female convicts. They were distributed as follows throughout the ships:

| | Convicts | |
Vessel	Male	Female
The Surprise	256	—
Neptune	424	78
Scarborough	259	—

Of these convicts quite a large number of the men came from Wales and four of the seventy-eight women aboard the *Neptune* had been tried in Wales. They were Sarah Evans and Grace Jones who were tried at Denbigh in 1786, Martha Morgan from Pembrokeshire and Margaret Clark from Radnorshire. Another Pembrokeshire woman, Jane Codd, seems to have actually embarked but then to have been transferred, probably through ill health, to a later sailing. In the case of the Second Fleet there is a great disparity between the numbers who embarked and the numbers disembarking in New South Wales. The Second Fleet's mortality rate was the highest in the history of transportation to Australia. Of the 1,000-odd convicts who sailed, 267 died on the voyage, i.e. 256 men and 11 women. Nearly 450 needed medical treatment when they reached Sydney and many did not survive much longer.

If one examines this voyage, especially that of the *Neptune*, on which the Welsh women sailed, one sees a tale of corruption and tragedy. The ships were equipped by private contractors and the important point to note is that these people were in this venture for a profit. In earlier times when contractors handled the transportation of convicts to America the contractors were paid according to the number of convicts they safely *landed*. In this way they had a vested interest in the health of the prisoners. But on the Australian run the contractors were paid according to the number of convicts *embarked*. They therefore had no interest in keeping the convicts fit and well. In fact, quite the contrary was the case, the more who died, the less mouths there were to feed and the more profits to be had. The master of the convict vessel *Neptune*, Donald Trail, in league with the contractors, held back food from the convicts and sold the stores, which he had saved, at a high price in Australia.

The convicts on the Second Fleet, especially those on Trail's ship, were starving. Scurvy and other diseases were rampant and the prisoners became emaciated. As an observer noted, 'The slave trade is merciful compared to what I have seen in this fleet.' In addition to the lack of food, the prisoners were treated with an amazing severity. The contractors thought it safest to keep the convicts in irons, which were not struck off until a few days before reaching Australia. Add to this the problem of vessels taking in water and the horrific picture of life aboard the Second Fleet begins to take shape. When the whole business was investigated it emerged that, 'Sometimes for days, nay, for a considerable time together they have been to the middle in water, chained together, hand and leg, even the sick not exempted, nay, many died with the chains upon them.' The largest number of complaints had come from the women aboard the *Neptune*, Trail's ship. Trail, however, escaped public prosecution and was later appointed to a government post at the Cape.

When the Second Fleet sailed into Sydney harbour it presented a vile sight. The Reverend Richard Johnson, on visiting the all-male convict vessel *The Surprise* in the harbour wrote:

> I beheld a sight truly shocking to the feelings of humanity, a great number of them laying some half and others nearly quite naked without either bed or bedding unable to turn or help themselves. Spoke to them as I passed along but the smell was so offensive I could scarcely bear it.

He planned to board the *Neptune* but knowing her to be, as he says, still more wretched, he did not attempt it. As for the state of the poor people when they attempted to disembark, Johnson wrote in utter shock:

> The landing of these people was truly affecting and shocking, great numbers were not able to walk, nor to move hand or foot; such were slung over the ship's side in the same manner as they would sling a cask, a box or anything of that nature. Upon being brought up to the open air some fainted, some died upon the deck and others in the boat before they reached the shore. When come on shore many were not able to walk, to stand, or to stir themselves in the least, hence some were led by others. Some creeped upon their hands and knees, and some were carried upon the backs of others.

All were in an indescribably filthy state, 'covered', as Johnson said, 'almost with their own nastiness, their heads, bodies, clothes, blankets, all full of filth and lice.'

It is not possible to look in detail at every voyage on which Welsh convict women sailed throughout a period of over sixty years but it is useful to survey the voyages over this long period through looking at certain aspects. The aspects which call for attention are the amount of space allotted to convicts, the segregation of prisoners, convict rations, clothing, health, occupation on the voyage, sexual abuse, conduct of prisoners and punishments for misconduct and, finally, the children of convict mothers on board.

The prison was usually situated in the 'tween decks. On the *Neptune* it was on the third or orlop deck and was 75 feet long with a height of *c.* 5½ feet under the beams or 6½ feet between them. There were rows of cabins, each 6 feet square. Strong bulkheads, studded with nails, cut off

Caged prisoners en route for Australia
Radio Times Hulton Picture Library

the prison quarters. A new design of 1817 altered the prison by dividing it into three distinct areas separated by bars. The aim was the separation of hardened prisoners from young ones, whilst still allowing ventilation. A description of this type of prison comes from Surgeon Cunningham:

> 'Two rows of sleeping berths, one above the other', he says, 'extended on each side of the between-decks, each berth being 6 feet square, and calculated to hold four convicts, every one thus possessing 18 inches square space to sleep in—and ample space, too! The hospital is in the fore-part of the ship; with a bulkhead across, separating it from the prison, having two doors with locks to keep out intruders; while a separate prison is built for the boys, to cut off all intercourse between them and the men. Strong wooden stanchions, thickly studded with nails, are fixed round the fore and main hatchways, between decks, in each of which is a door with three padlocks, to let the convicts out and in, and secure them at night. The convicts by these means have no access to the hold through the prison, a ladder being placed in each hatchway, for them to go up and down by, which is pulled on deck at night.'

Thereafter there was little change in design and throughout the transportation era the ships were cramped and ill ventilated.

Precisely how much space the convicts had tended to vary from ship to ship. In 1791 the *Pitt* was clearly overloaded. An investigation of conditions aboard showed a 6 foot cube was allocated to every eight male convicts and, 'if a sickness should happen, a sick and a healthy person must touch each other.' The women were placed in three separate quarters aboard the *Pitt*. Two of these were rooms measuring *c*. 6½ feet by less than 8 feet and the third and largest room was just over 13 feet long and 8 feet wide. This last room was designed to accommodate twenty-seven women. In fact, some male convicts were removed from the vessel before it sailed because of overcrowding but more women were actually put on board. Fifty-eight women, and not the original forty-seven, sailed. There may have been an extra cabin provided but there is no reference to it. Within this group was a solitary Welsh woman—Ann Glossop from Montgomeryshire. Not surprisingly there was a high death toll on this packed vessel and nine of the female prisoners died. Ann Glossop may well have been one of them since I have found no further trace of her.

Other ships were better than the *Pitt*. The *Royal Admiral* sailed the same year, and although larger and roomier than the *Pitt* she embarked sixty-two less prisoners. There were several Welsh women aboard— Rachel Davies from Carmarthen, who had originally been placed on the unsafe vessel, *Kitty*, was on the *Royal Admiral*—she was being trans-

The Pitt which carried Welsh women to New South Wales
National Maritime Museum, Greenwich

ported because she had broken into a house at Llangunnor and stolen used clothes and a cheap necklace. Sarah Burt and Mary Jenkins from Glamorgan were there too. Sarah had originally been sentenced to death for her part in a burglary, but her sentence was commuted. Mary Jenkins had stolen goods valued at ninepence. But even if the *Royal Admiral* appears excellent in comparison to the *Pitt* she was still very crowded. Governor Philip wrote to London in these words:

> Of the convicts embarked 10 men and 2 women died and 4 children were born, one of whom died . . . 72 men, 11 women and 5 children have been landed sick. I think the people have been too much crowded on board this ship.

Actually it was considered quite reasonable to allocate a space 6 feet by 6 feet to four convicts. This seems appalling to us, but one has to remember that sailors too had very cramped quarters. But throughout the whole era of transportation right down to the 1850s, when Britain was showing off to the world by staging the Great Exhibition, her convicts sailed in cramped conditions. The worst part of the voyage, because of the overcrowding, was in the tropics and the following description of this living hell comes from an articulate Irish political prisoner, John Boyle O'Reilly:

> 'When the ship was becalmed in the tropics', he wrote, 'the suffering of the imprisoned wretches in the steaming and crowded hold

103

was piteous to see. They were so packed that free movement was impossible. The best thing to do was to sit each on his or her berth, and suffer in patience. The air was stifling and oppressive. There was no draught through the barred hatches. The deck above them was blazing hot. The pitch dropped from the seams, and burned their flesh as it fell. There was only one word spoken or thought— one yearning idea in every mind—water, cool water to slake the parching thirst. Two pints of water a day were served out to each convict—a quart of half-putrid and blood-warm liquid. It was a woeful sight to see the thirsty souls devour this allowance as soon as their hot hands seized the vessel. Day in and day out, the terrible calm held the ship, and the consuming heat sapped the lives of the pent-up convicts . . . Hideous incidents filled the days and nights as the convict ship sailed southward with her burden of disease and death. The mortality among the convicts was frightful. Weakened and depressed by the long drought, the continuous heat, and the poisonous atmosphere, they succumbed to the fever in its first stages.'

On the whole, however, there were certain clear improvements over the years. Ironing was less frequent, prisoners were allowed more on deck and the faster times achieved by later vessels at least cut down the length of time at sea.

At first, little thought was given to the notion of segregating prisoners. In the early years male and female convicts were transported on the same vessels and this was justified as being the normal practice on board slave ships. Not until 1811 did the segregation of male and female convicts on separate ships become the rule. As for separating prisoners of different characters and different degrees of criminality, there was far less success. Elizabeth Fry saw an opportunity in this direction when she boarded the *Maria* in 1818. Distressed at the sight of so many women and children milling around and herded together below deck and knowing that they were to be grouped into messes of six for the voyage, she intervened. She and her companions did the grouping and 'as far as possible those whose ages or criminality were similar were placed together.' But quite how effective this type of segregation was on the voyage is rather doubtful and association between various types of convicts was not really curbed. As late as 1837 when Dr. Morgan Price, a naval surgeon, answered questions put to him in an inquiry, his replies show inadequate separation of prisoners. The interview proceeded as follows:

Have you had the means of classifying them on board ship, or have they had unrestrained intercourse? Partly so, but not altogether so well as I could wish.

Female convicts in a crowded hold
National Library of Australia

What means of classification have you on board ship? Schooling is
the principal point; those who can read and write have been
separated as much as possible.
*Has the separation been complete, or have they still had inter-
course one with another generally during the passage?*—Always
intercourse; we could not avoid that.
*Have you been able to make any classification founded on the
character of the prisoners?* Not satisfactorily.
*Have you had the means of observing whether their conduct has
improved or deteriorated during the voyage?* Not all; with every
means we can possibly adopt through the voyage, I consider they
are as bad at the end of the voyage as in the first instance.
Do you think they are worse? They certainly do not improve.

The mess was the basic unit in which the convicts lived, ate and slept.
The surgeon, who came to have overall responsibility for convicts, was
authorised by the government to encourage orderly and clean messes
among the women by giving rewards. The cleanest mess of the day was
given a gratuity of 1 ounce of tea and 2 ounces of sugar. Actually each
mess of female convicts was given a luxury not shared by the male convicts. This was a 'kettle to serve as a tea pot' to each mess and a drinking mug for every woman.

The rations with which convicts were provided were on the whole
satisfactory. To each mess of six, every week the following supplies
were allocated:

> 20 lbs. bread.
> 12 lbs. flour
> 16 lbs. beef
> 6 lbs. pork
> 12 pints of peas
> 1 lb. butter
> 8 oz. rice
> 1½ lbs. suet
> 3 lbs. raisins
> 6 pints oatmeal
> 4 ozs. sugar

This was the regulation issue from 1812 onwards. The supervision of
rations was a duty of the surgeon. In orders dated 1835 the surgeon was
commanded to make sure that the convicts all received their due
rations, that their food was properly cooked and regularly served and
that each convict received her/his water ration. As a further precaution,
it was stated that two convicts, one from each of two messes in rotation,
should be present when the rations were issued. If the surgeon noticed

that the convicts were not eating or were wasting any particular item it was to be withdrawn. The water allowance, which he supervised, was not to exceed one gallon per day in the tropics and six pints the rest of the time. The surgeon was also to ensure that each convict received one ounce of lemon juice and sugar which was either to be taken as a sherbet or mixed in with the wine allowance. Its inclusion was, of course, necessary to prevent scurvy. One other function of the surgeon related to food rations was the prevention of corruption and swindling the convicts of their stores. He was, as his orders state, to be present when each new cask of food was opened:

> He is to attend the opening of every cask of provisions issued from the King's stores which is to be brought upon deck for the purpose, and note its state and condition, note number and contents in the journal he is directed to keep by the 37th Article of these instructions. Two harness casks, with padlocks, (one for beef and one for pork) are supplied to the ship, into which the contents of each cask of provisions are to be put, and the keys given in charge of the mates. At the conclusion of the voyage he is to survey the remains of provisions on board, and report in what state they may be found previous to their being landed.

This careful supervision had been proved necessary. One has only to think of the villainous Trail on the Second Fleet to see the need for these regulations. Other abuses included the purchase of the prisoners' salt meat rations by the master or officers at a very low price and often payment was made in tobacco or tea. This diminution of the salt intake was not a good thing in the tropics. This type of abuse and the giving of short weight were to a certain extent checked, but some ill-dealing did continue. Mary Davies sentenced in 1826 to seven years' transportation by the Pembrokeshire Great Sessions, sailed aboard *The Harmony* in 1827 to New South Wales. The master, Captain Middleton, was accused by the surgeon of short serving the rations to the eighty women aboard. He was apparently barred from the convict service for this.

The rags and tatters which convict women wore on the First and Second Fleets were replaced in the nineteenth century by regulation issues of garments. It is not certain what the early uniform was, but it is known that it was inadequate, especially on vessels leaving in the winter. The government was long prejudiced against the issue of warm woollen or flannel garments on the grounds, it was said, that these would harbour disease. This seems derisory in view of the other conditions. By the mid 1820s the following list of garments per woman was issued. This list is that to be supplied to Eleanor Williams of Caernarvonshire:

Clothing for each Convict:

One New Woollen Jacket or Gown.

One Do. Cotton Do.

One Do. Cotton Petticoat.

Two Do. Flannel Do.

Three Do. Shifts

Two Do. Neckhandkerchiefs, Coloured.

Three Do. Pair of Stockings (Two Pair of which Worsted.)

Two Do. Pair of Shoes.

Clothing for each Convict

One New Woollen Jacket or Gown
One New Cotton Jacket or Gown
One New Cotton Petticoat
Two New Flannel Petticoats
Three New Shifts
Two New Neckhandkerchiefs, Coloured.
Three New Pair of Stockings (Two Pair of which Worsted)
Two New Pair of Shoes

By the 1830s the clothing list had changed slightly and a linen cap and check apron was added to it. Each woman was also issued with a strong hessian apron and a very useful item, a bag in which to store her clothes. These two were not provided by the government but by Elizabeth Fry's charitable organisation. The careful thought of this body is also reflected in their gift to prisoners of a comb, a ball of string and a pair of stay laces. By the 1840s the government had introduced a further refinement in the clothing of women by issuing white jackets and checked aprons for the tropics. It is said that the women on board the ships visited by Mrs. Fry's Ladies' Committee took far greater care over their cleanliness and personal appearance than did those on earlier voyages. We have a cameo picture of the appearance of women on board the *Rajah*. This comes from a 'female of superior attainments' who had previously been a prison officer in England and was, voluntarily, accompanying the convict women. She wrote to Mrs. Pryor, who had visited eighty convict ships and who was a good friend of Elizabeth Fry, in these words:

> I must again dear Madam for a few minutes resume my pen in order to depict to you the scene of yesterday. It was, as you will imagine from our latitude, excessively hot: but an awning was fixed up and gave the deck the appearance of a church . . . The women for the first time put on the cool white jackets and checked aprons provided for them and I cannot tell you how really picturesque and neat they looked from their uniformity of dress.

The women were provided with more and better clothes than they had ever owned in their lives and many of them were being transported for stealing old garments of less value!

Convict ships were not healthy places. The vessels of the Second and indeed Third Fleets were rife with disease and dirt. Dysentry, typhoid, scurvy and smallpox were all common diseases on convict transports especially in the early years. Poor ventilation, the embarkation of already sick prisoners, the wetness and dirt of many ships produced breeding grounds for disease. But again, as time progressed over the period when transportation was employed as a punishment, there was an improvement in cleanliness and in convict health. Whereas a horrific mortality rate of one death in about every three convicts prevailed in the 1790s, by the 1820s or 1830s it was more like about one in every twenty-five. These are still appalling figures. But in fact the worst death rates had been for male convicts in the early period and this was the area of greatest improvement. Yet improvements though there were, here are some examples of mortality rates on vessels, carrying, among others, Welsh women to Tasmania in the 1830s and 1840s.

Year of Arrival	Ship	Number embarked	Deaths	One death in every so many convicts
1833	*Fanny*	106	8	1 in 13
1833	*William Bryan*	130	7	1 in 19
1843	*Garland Grove*	191	8	1 in 24
1849	*Cadet*	150	7	1 in 21

The improvements which were introduced were largely due to the appointment of naval surgeons as surgeon-superintendents on convict transports. Many of these were conscientious men who took their duties very seriously. Among these duties was responsibility for cleanliness on board. The instructions to surgeons issued in the 1830s included:

> He is to take care that the convicts' berths are kept clean and as airy as possible; that the greatest cleanliness be observed among the convicts, both in their persons and habits, and in the hospital; and that as much ventilation be used as may be consistent with due warmth. As it is very essential that damp should be prevented by every practicable means, he is to cause the swing stoves, which are supplied to the ship, to be frequently used in different parts of the prison and the hospital, for the purpose of promoting warmth, dryness and a circulation of air; and he is to cause the two lanterns, which the owners are bound to provide, to be kept burning in the fore and main hatchways, during the darkness of night, for the purpose of preventing every irregularity.

He was also to ensure that water closets between decks were available and kept in good order:

> He is to select a set of men from among the convicts, in order that one may be placed as a guard over each water closet between decks, to prevent anything being thrown into it that would tend to choke the pipe, and to see that it be cleansed by letting water pass through from the cistern every time it is used. These guards are to

The bath aboard the *Success*
Radio Times Hulton Picture Library

be relieved at fixed periods according to his discretion; and he is to cause the convicts to use the seats of ease on deck as much as possible, in preference to the water-closets.

Efforts were apparently made, at least in later years, to see that the prisoners themselves were clean. The provision of the gruesome looking bath (*see illustration*) would have been a step in this direction. The idea was that the prisoner should be put in, the grating closed, and then an attendant would scrub the prisoner's back! This sort of measure and the solicitous assistance of Elizabeth Fry's Ladies did lead to a general improvement in convicts' cleanliness and appearance.

Of course, a central part of the Surgeon's duty was the care of the sick. According to his orders, he was to make a daily inspection of the convicts to detect any symptons of 'fever, flux, scurvy or any other complaint' in an effort to stop the spread of disease. Infected convicts were to be removed to the ship's hospital and 'there their persons to be thoroughly cleansed and their clothing to be washed in boiling water or fumigated before it is stowed away.' He was to appoint other trustworthy and fit convicts as nurses. The government provided a fixed list of medical comforts for every 100 convicts and a list of hospital equipment, as set out below:

Description	Males	Females
MEDICAL COMFORTS:		
Preserved meats, including soup*	75 lbs.	131¼ lbs.
Lemon juice	648 —	648 —
Sugar to mix with it	648 —	648 —
		(None, as these
Tea	6¾ lbs.	(articles form
Sugar	48 lbs.	(part of the
		(rations
Scotch barley	60 —	60 —
Ginger	4 oz.	4 oz.
Red port wine	9 bott.	18 bott.
Vinegar	7½ gall.	7½ gall.

*A pint of soup is equal to a pound of preserved meats.

Note: These comforts, when necessary in sickness, are to be issued to all other persons as well as convicts to whom King's provisions are issued.

Medicines as per List, transmitted to the Surgeon.

Description	Males	Females
HOSPITAL FURNITURE:		
Flannel trowsers	4 pairs	
— waistcoats	4 No.	
Bed gowns, calico		4 No.
Petticoats		4 No.
Night caps	3	8
Towels	6	8
Child-bed linen		6 sets
Pillow cases	4	16
Sheets	4 prs.	8 prs.
Tea-kettles	2 No.	2 No.
Drinking mugs	6 —	
Sea boilers, 6 quarts		2 —
,, ,, 4 ,,	1 —	2 —
,, ,, 2 ,,	2 —	
Saucepans 1 quart	2 —	2 —
,, 1 pint	2 —	2 —
Wood cradles 2 No.)		
Night chair 1 —)		
Close-stool pans 2 No.) To		
Bed pans 2 —) each		
Urinals 2 —) ship		
Spitting pots 1 —)		
Bath 1 —)		

It is interesting to note that the women received more port wine, meat and bedding than did the men. The explanation for this is very likely that these provisions for women were also to cover the children on board. One hundred convict women could well have thirty to forty children with them.

Government instructions to the surgeons read well on paper, but not every single surgeon carried them out: one was accused of visiting the prison only twice in two months. The journey to Australia continued to be quite harrowing and although steps were taken to prevent infected people embarking the surgeons were told that bodily infirmity was no excuse for a convict not embarking. We know that on the *Garland Grove*, a vessel with Welsh women aboard, one of the women who died was ill on embarkation. Cholera broke out on the transport *Fanny* before she sailed in July 1832. An extra surgeon was put aboard and the outbreak was contained, but thirty women developed scurvy and eight of her 106 convict women died from other diseases. On board this vessel were Ellin Parry sentenced in Denbighshire and Ann Tippings from

Monmouthshire. Aboard the *Sovereign* which arrived in Tasmania in 1827, none of the eighty-seven women died but Catherine Jones, a servant in husbandry, sentenced to transportation for life by a Caernarvonshire court, was too ill on arrival to answer questions for the records. Ann Morgan, tried in Pembrokeshire in 1827, died the next year aboard *The Borneo* bound for Van Diemen's Land.

The journey to Australia was a long one and, when not frightful, it could be very tedious, especially for the female convicts. Sometimes male convicts were employed in duties related to the sailing of the ship, but normally women were not. Yet obviously, it was in the interests of good order to provide some kind of worthwhile occupation. The prevailing pastime seems to have been gambling—cards, dice, pitch and toss. There are tales of country bumpkins being taken in by city slickers and gambling away their rations for days on end. This was a deplorable state of affairs. One ship's master, Captain Aitken, of the *Juliana* exploited the situation. He kept women at work throughout the passage making shirts. He gave them a pittance for their labour and sold the shirts at a great profit at Port Jackson, New South Wales. Yet there was something in Aitken's idea and one suspects many women were just happy to have something to do. The British government could have learned from Aitken, but instead it was Elizabeth Fry who again showed concern. She thought up a clever scheme. She went to the 'Manchester' (i.e. textile) houses in London and asked them for any old scraps of material. They gladly gave them to her. She then set the women aboard the *Maria* to making patchwork items. Not only did this provide the women with a useful pastime, it also earned them a little money. When in 1819 the *Wellington* put into Rio en route to New South Wales, the patchwork quilts were sold at a guinea each. Heaven knows the convict women would need that guinea when they arrived in Australia!

In time the government followed Elizabeth Fry's idea and issued the convicts with the following materials. In the list below the patchwork pieces were to be divided between 100 convict women and each woman received the packet of sewing implements:

FOR FEMALE CONVICTS ONLY
Articles of Haberdashery etc., for Work on the Voyage

Patch pieces	200 lbs.
Packages	100 No.

Each Package containing:

Scissors	1 pair
Black and white sewing cotton	1½ oz.

Mixed pins	1
Thimble	1 No.
Bodkin	1
Tape	1 piece
Black and brown thread	2 hanks
Laces	2 No.
Needles, small	100
Needles, large	8
Black worsted	1 oz.
Check work-bag	1 No.
Small bag to contain the articles	1 —

Note: The articles are to be issued for the purpose of providing them with constant employment. Every convict who conducts herself properly is to be allowed, on her arrival in the colony, to dispose of her work as she may think proper. This indulgence is not, however, to be allowed to those who behave disorderly, but their work is to be disposed of as the governor may direct. Notice to this effect is to be placed in the prison for the information of the convicts.

Not only were women convicts provided with a useful pastime, as a result of an initiative of Elizabeth Fry and the Ladies' Committee, but another benefit stemmed from the intervention of this charitable body. The Ladies took an interest in the education of the convicts. They were less concerned with improving convict career prospects than with enabling them to read the scriptures and thereby attain salvation. A number of missionaries and well intentioned ladies sailed on the convict ships in later years and spent much time teaching the scriptures and reading and writing to the convicts. It was an act of great devotion on their part, given the hazards of a long sea voyage. In 1835 the *George Hibbert* sailed to New South Wales. She was carrying 144 women, who included Mary Lewis, tried at Carmarthen, Jane Isaac tried in Glamorgan for stealing two pieces of flannel, and finally Catherine Pugh, who stole a curtain and some household linen and who was tried in Merionethshire. On board the vessel were Mr. and Mrs. Saunders, missionaries, who were given a free passage in exchange for providing the convicts with religious instructions. These two sent home reports and a letter of theirs, dated two days after they had crossed the equator, showed that they were holding daily church services and two on Sunday and that they had set up a school for the children and the women. This school was held on deck, weather permitting. In fact, a violent storm off Tristan d'Acunha had halted its progress for a while. As a testimony to the Saunders' work the ship's master, Captain Livesay, wrote that some of the women, who had embarked unable to read or write, 'have left her

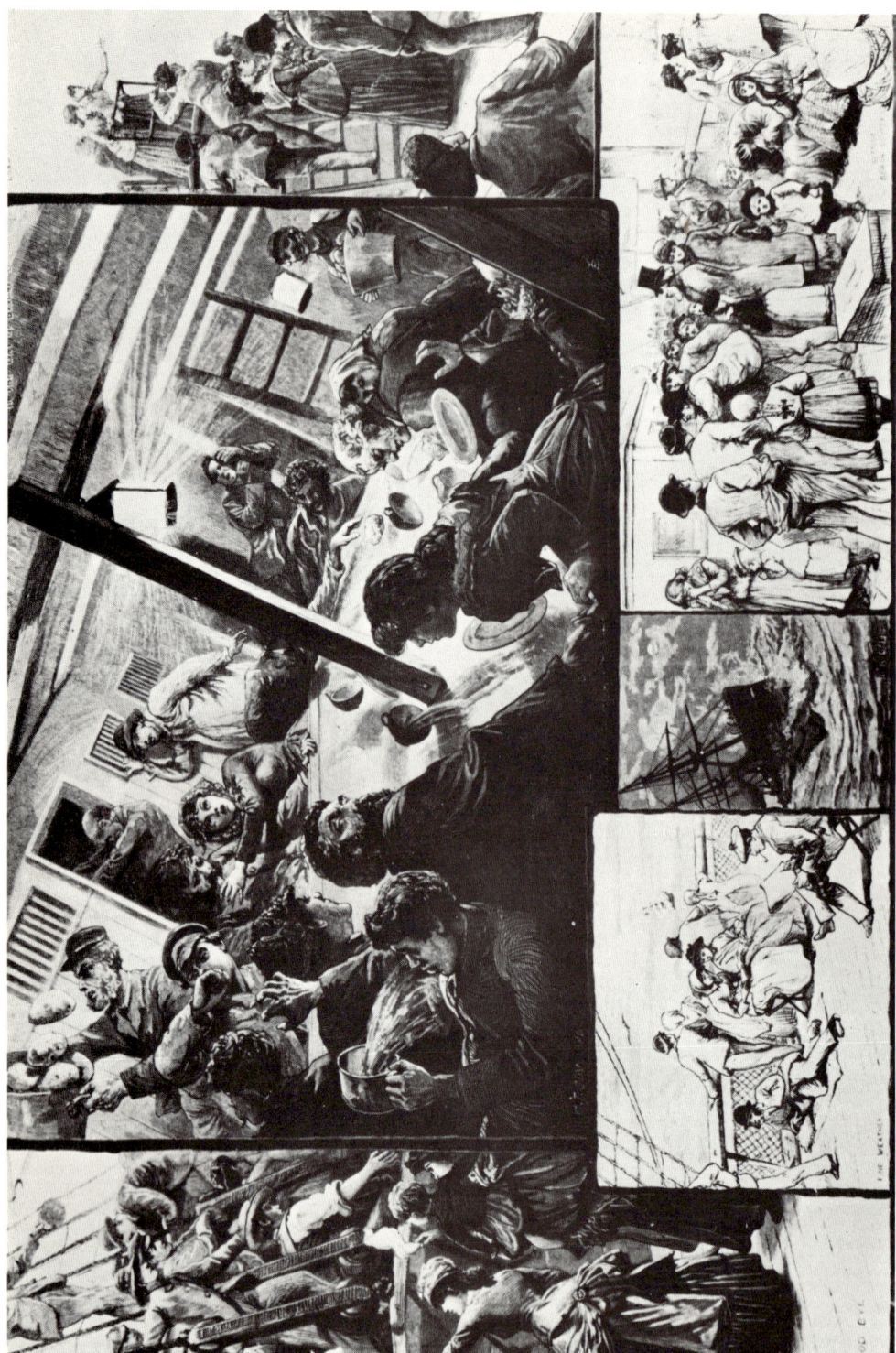

Large inset: emigrants to Australia in rough weather
Australian Information Service, London

well capable of doing both.' Likewise the surgeon aboard the *Earl of Liverpool* wrote to Elizabeth Fry:

> Having lately returned from New South Wales, after the termination of my duties as surgeon superintendent of The Earl of Liverpool female convict ship, I know it will be pleasing to you to learn that during the voyage to the Colony the behaviour of the women was quiet and orderly, and, with a very few exceptions, I may say exemplary. Having now performed two voyages in charge of female convict ships, I cannot but express a very favourable opinion of the good effects arising from the endeavours of the members of the Ladies' Association, to afford instruction to the prisoners, as well as employment, during the voyage. The patchwork supplied them, with books etc., kept them pretty much occupied; and the school established on board was regularly attended by all the children, and many of the prisoners. The system of moral discipline followed on board was that of strictness, tempered with kindness and every opportunity taken to impress upon them the value of an approving conscience, and to raise them in their own estimation, by showing them that they were cared for. The difference in the habits and manners of the prisoners from Newgate, and those from places in the country where no system of prison discipline was followed, was a subject of common remark by the officers of the ship and myself, and cannot but be gratifying to the members of the Ladies' Association, as well as hold out the strongest inducements to continue their useful labours for the reformation of female prisoners.

Finally, a detailed account of life aboard a convict vessel in the 1840s survives. The ship was the *Garland Grove* and the writer Miss Elizabeth Lang Grindod. In an account sent to Elizabeth Fry, Miss Grindod relates that her ship had arrived safely after 'an agreeable voyage of 110 days.' Her adjective is somewhat surprising since eight convict women had died on the journey. Miss Grindod was accompanied by a Miss McLarene but the latter was totally indisposed, probably by seasickness, for the first fortnight of the voyage and so they delayed the start of a school until she had found her sea legs. As Miss Grindod relates:

> We selected two school mistresses and determined to do without monitors. Though it was an addition to our labours, we found it an advantage, as it prevented many disputes that might otherwise have arisen twixt the prisoners. There were only seven of the children old enough to be taught their letters: these could read very nicely when we reached the end of our voyage. Amongst the

women were fifteen who were totally unacquainted with the alphabet: ten of them proved apt and diligent scholars; one was upwards of 50 years old. Some could read but imperfectly and we had the pleasure of seeing them improve, others could read but not write and they gladly embraced the opportunity of learning.

On that voyage of the *Garland Grove* were six Welsh women. They were Ann Williams, tried Anglesey, Ellen Davies, tried Denbigh, Sarah Davies and Eliza Wheeler tried in Glamorgan and Mary Williams and Charity Hogg both of whom were tried in Monmouthshire. When it came to Miss Grindod's classes Eliza Wheeler, a 20-year-old dairy maid from Herefordshire, would have been classified as a reader but not a writer. Whereas Ann Williams from Anglesey would have been at a disadvantage: she could read and write in Welsh but she knew no English. She must have been very lonely. Actually the two women behaved very differently on board. Eliza is described as 'a very hard working girl. Messwoman: clean and tidy.' Whereas Ann is dismissed in a single word—'bad'.

The two ladies organised the school to begin at 9.00 a.m., when all the women, apart from those cleaning the prison, assembled. Miss McLarene instructed a group in religion while Miss Grindod took thirty women for one and half hours in a writing lesson. The writing class was followed by a two hour class in reading. At noon the convict women took their dinner break. Miss McLarene supervised the women who were at work on the top deck, presumably washing it, and constantly pointed out to the idle the advantages of industry. Meanwhile Miss Grindod was helping in the ship's hospital. After dinner the women were left to their own devices and Miss Grindod notes the pleasure she felt as she listened to a convict woman reading aloud to her companions. There was a library on board and its use was permitted as a reward for good conduct. As in prison libraries, the books were hardly compelling reading. There were volumes on travel(!), history, religion and serious poetry but 'no novels, plays or other improper books.' At five o'clock the women had tea and at six o'clock they were locked up for the night. The two Christian ladies went below and held a short service for them.

One often gets the impression that the convicts were glad of the diversion provided by the Christian volunteers. I am sure that the mere presence of missionaries on board was a good thing as they frequently complained about abuses and were known to publicise them. Yet just how sincere the convicts were in their response to these devout people is a little doubtful. Some missionaries and well intentioned ships officers were clearly very gullible. One surgeon, Dr. Reid of the *Morley* (1820) was quite satisfied with the following performance from a convict woman. 'Nancy Reid, a convict of notorious character', he wrote, 'gave evidence of satisfactory reform by reciting a hymn which I had given her to commit to memory a few days before.' But the two ladies aboard the *Garland Grove* were more perceptive. Writing about a woman who died on the vessel, they said that they had taken every opportunity to save her and she appeared to cherish their words in their presence but Miss Grindod discovered after her death, that 'she turned all that had been said to her to ridicule. She died as she had lived, without the fear of God.' As for the problem of swearing and the use of profane oaths among the women, Miss Grindod realised, 'the habit was so confirmed that I am fully persuaded that nothing less than a work of grace in their hearts could eradicate the evil.'

Female convicts for much of the period, when transportation was used as a punishment, endured a very long voyage, cramped and often wet conditions, close confinement in small prisons below deck and were exposed to a considerable risk of disease. All this the male convicts also suffered. But the one additional problem for the female convict was that of persistent sexual abuse. The danger of rape or enforced cohabitation was almost always present on the voyage especially in the early part of the period. One should remember that half of the Welsh women were *not* prostitutes. They were often powerless against unsolicited advances and since they were all, very sweepingly, considered whores, their protests counted for nothing. Of course, it would be naive to say that all advances came from the men. Many of the big city women had been 'on the town' for years and were just glad of any opportunity to make a bit of money. But for many women there simply was no choice but to submit to the men . . . officers, crew, or, later, to masters in Australia. Yet nearly all writers exonerate the men completely and place the whole blame for the sexual abuses aboard the ship on the women themselves. Surgeon White in his *Journal of A Voyage to New South Wales* epitomises this one-sided attitude and places the whole responsibility for promiscuity on the women. He wrote:

> The hatches over the place where they were confined could not suffer to lay off, during the night without a promiscuous intercourse between them (the women) and the sea men and marines.

He explains that the blame clearly attached to the women since:

> In some ships, the desire of the woman to be with the men was so uncontrollable that neither shame or the form of punishment could deter them from making their way through the bulkhead to the apartments assigned to the seamen.

The poor seamen are shown as victims and the women as the ardent pursuers! This may have happened on some occasions, but there is hardly any reference to the reverse situation. Only a few glimpses of the sexual abuse of the women comes through. As we have seen aboard the *Lady Juliana* in 1791, a mariner, John Nicol, wrote 'Every man on board took a wife from among the convicts, *they nothing loathe*.' Of course, he did not mean 'wife' and how do we know that they were 'nothing loathe'? We only have Nicol's word. The following observer seems a reliable witness. Mr. W. H. R. Brown stated before the Select Committee inquiring into the State of Gaols in 1829, 'the youngest and handsomest women were selected from the other convicts and sent on board by order of the master . . . for the vilest purposes.' Sometimes the voice of a convict woman herself survives, like that of the woman who accused a surgeon of being 'a poxy bloodletter who seduced innocent girls while treating them for the fever and using his surgery as a floating whore house.'

Certainly, convict women had little control over their own fate. A good example of this is the case of the vessel *Lady Shore*. The military guard on board, a real rabble, seized control of the vessel and made for South America where the women were distributed. Nobody knows what became of the women in Monte Video.

There were attempts to check what is always called prostitution on board. The mere choice of word puts the blame one hundred per cent on the women! On the transport *Friendship* in 1817 and on the *Janus* in 1820 'prostitution' was so rife that an inquiry followed. It is noteworthy that both ships had missionaries on board and that these people were prepared to make a public issue of what was fairly normal practice. One suspects the government held inquiries to stop the missionaries making more fuss. The laissez-faire and disinterested attitude of the government is summed up in the comments by Mr. Justice Field, who arrived to take up high office in Australia, on the *Lord Melville* in 1817. He conceded that the surgeon superintendent might have reformed the practice, but it was scarcely worth it and also almost impossible to prevent connection between the men and the women. Even with so distinguished a passenger as Field aboard, the captain and surgeon could not check abuse! By the 1830s the problem of prostitution or sexual abuse or rape was still there and the government was taking more action. The surgeon was to give certificates of good behaviour to the mates who abstained from liaisons with the women and thereby enable them to gain a cash reward. The order reads:

> If he be appointed to a ship in which female convicts are to be embarked, he is to use his utmost endeavours to prevent their prostitution with the officers, passengers or crew; showing a good example himself in this particular, and not failing to report to the governor any instance of improper intercourse with the women

which may be detected. It is necessary the governor's certificate should be explicit in stating that he is satisfied every practicable means have been adopted to prevent prostitution; and as an inducement to the mates of the ship to support the surgeon superintendent in his exertions to attain the object, a gratuity will be paid to the chief mate of 20 l. and to the second and third mates of 15 l. each, on their producing a certificate from him on the termination of the voyage, that they have conducted themselves to his satisfaction.

Sometimes 'prostitution' was the cause of other troubles. A good case in point is the voyage of the vessel *Brothers,* which sailed into Tasmania in April 1824. Incidentally this ship carried the only woman sentenced by a Cardiganshire court to transportation. She was Eleanor James aged 24 and designated as a 'thief from childhood' but who was not, as far as is known, a prostitute. She had 'won her passage' by stealing clothes from a house in Tremain. The journey of the *Brothers* lasted 131 days (4½ months) but only one prisoner died on the voyage. This particular passage is, in fact, notorious. The ship's surgeon was one James Hall, an officer who had made previous voyages on transport vessels and who was known as a 'meddlesome and litigious individual'. He tried to suppress prostitution on board the *Brothers* and within one week of sailing he was seriously assaulted by six of the convict women. These, Hall maintained, were acting under the orders of the chief mate. Whether Eleanor James was involved in this is not known but on arrival in Tasmania her conduct on board ship was described as 'disorderly'.

When examining the issue of prostitution, one comes up against the question of how the women behaved on the voyage. It was one of the duties of the surgeon-superintendents to write a report on each woman at the end of the voyage. Elizabeth Fry's Ladies were always stressing the value of a good report since it helped the women to get work in Australia and the surgeon urged 'a cheerful compliance with the regulations.' Some Welsh women obviously did comply with fairly good grace and some won glowing reports. Mary Ann Morgan of Glamorgan aboard the *Elizabeth and Henry* in 1846-7 was described as 'very well behaved and industrious.' Ann Jenkins, a laundress from Pembrokeshire, who was tried in Brecon, was in the words in the surgeon's report 'industrious and well behaved: a messwoman; can recommend her.' Elizabeth Morris of Radnorshire aboard the *Sea Queen* was praised because she had done duty as cook on board. Quite a few others won reports of very good, good and orderly. But not everybody behaved so compliantly. The surgeon aboard the *Stately* in 1849 could not say better of Elizabeth Williams of Merthyr Tydfil than 'very indifferent'. Whilst the surgeon of the *Edward* condemned 18-year-old Swansea

Irons as used on a convict ship

woman Ann Evans as 'bad, a thief'. Margaret Presdee, a 22-year-old cook from Caernarvon, won the surgeon's disapproval and was described as a 'very bad character'. Others from Wales were described as slovenly, malicious, noisy and indolent. Finally, Ann Driffield, an older woman and a widow, whose crime was receiving stolen goods in Monmouthshire, sailed on board the *Tasmania*. She was 'one of the very worst on board.'

Punishments for misconduct were severe and some ships had a reputation for harsh punishments. The *Britannia* in 1796 was called a hell ship. Men on board received floggings of up to 800 lashes and women were placed in a neck yoke, their heads shaven and their legs ironed. Petty infringements of rules earned three to four dozen cuts with the cane. Yet another punishment was devised on board the *Lady Juliana*: recalcitrant women were made to wear a barrel, so they could neither lie nor sit down.

Accompanying their convict mothers, children too sailed to the Australian penal colonies. The regulations permitting children on the voyage stated:

> Children whose ages do not exceed, if boys 6 years and girls 10 years, will be allowed to accompany their mothers but if either of such convicts should have a child at the breast she must not be removed on board the said ship.

A convict woman could take her child or children with her, not knowing how she could support them, or, if she had a family who were agreeable, she could leave her children behind, knowing that she would probably never see them again. Most women had no choice and took their children with them. To give an example of the numbers involved on a trip, we see that the *George Hibbert* in 1834 had in addition to 150 convict women 41 children on board. The government provided these children with food and clothing on the voyage. Each male and female child was issued with the following:

CLOTHING FOR CHILDREN

Each Male		Each Female	
Kersey jackets	1 No.	Brown serge jackets	1 No.
Kersey waistcoats	1 —	— — petti-	
Kersey trowsers	1 pair	coats with bodies	1 No.
Striped cotton shirts	3 No.	Linen shifts	2 —
Worsted stockings	2 pair	— caps	1 —
Shoes	1 —	Worsted stockings	1 pair
Woollen caps	1 —	Shoes	1 —
Neck handkerchiefs	1 —	Neck handkerchiefs	1 No.

123

Note: The clothing for children is supplied in the proportion of one-third for males and two-thirds for females, the latter being suitable for young boys as well as girls.

Like their mothers, these children were provided with better clothes than they had ever before possessed or than their mothers had attempted to steal for them.

Some details survive about the identity of the children and their mothers. Margaret Philips, sentenced in Monmouthshire, aged 20 on arrival in Tasmania and a single woman, took her baby with her on the *Stately* in 1849. The baby, who was the son of a man with whom she had cohabited for three years, was named Charles. Rather puzzlingly, his age on arrival was just 7 months. Given the length of the voyage he must have been embarked at about 3 months and was therefore very clearly just a baby at the breast. Again Eleanor William's son, George, was only 8-months-old when he reached Tasmania on the *Emma Eugenia* in 1843. Some Welsh women brought several children with them. Elizabeth Thomas, a non-English speaker from Caernarvon, took two of her four children and Bridget Williams from Monmouthshire took three of her children.

It is a horrifying thought that these children shared the often abominable conditions aboard ship. Some, however, did not make it to the ships. Mary Thomas' baby died in gaol before she was removed from Beaumaris to the port. Other children died on the voyage and yet others were born.

Actually, there is little information about the children and how they passed the voyage. The Ladies' Committee set up schools for them on some ships. On the *Maria* in 1818, fourteen of the children were considered old enough for instruction. But we need to be aware that the modern concept of childhood as a separate and special period was not accepted in the eighteenth and early nineteenth centuries. Children were simply small people, who had to put up with the same hardships as adults. When Elizabeth Fry's colleague, Miss Neave, spoke about children to the 1837 commissioners, her concern was setting up an institute for 'wicked little girls', who would have to be punished, albeit differently from adults. Anyway, we should remember that people we would today regard as children were themselves sentenced to transportation. Fanny Bennett of Montgomeryshire was only in her early teens when she was sent to Tasmania. I have come across two young girls in Glamorgan who were aged 13 and 16 respectively and on whom sentence of transportation was passed. But apparently mercy prevailed here and they did not sail. When one finds this sort of treatment of children, or indeed, thinks of their employment in the mines, one

Sydney Cove in 1788

Australian Information Service, London

becomes aware that they were no special category. In fact, the Governor
of Millbank prison, Captain Groves, wrote:

> In 1844 I received 31 transports under 12 years of age; from 12 to
> 14 years of age 75 and from 14 to 17 233, making a total of 339
> under 17.

As the one English magistrate calmly wrote about very young girls
and boys, 'I often sentence a child to a month's imprisonment and to be
well whipped at the end of a fortnight, so as to keep the terror over his
mind for a fortnight.'

Between 1787 and 1852 many convict vessels carried women to New
South Wales and Tasmania. The complete list of vessels on which
Welsh women sailed is included in the Appendix. Some voyages,
however, stand out from the normal, if *any* convict voyage can be called
normal, and are clearly exceptional. Three voyages of vessels transpor-
ting Welsh women strike me as belonging in this category. They are the
voyages of the *Emu* in 1812, the *Kains* in 1830 and, most important of
all, that of the vessel *Amphitrite* in 1833.

In November 1812 the brig *Emu*, a vessel bought expressly for the
colonial service, set sail from England to New South Wales. She was
under the command of a Royal Navy Lieutenant, Alexander Bissett.
Her crew numbered 22 and it seems that she carried 49 convict women.
One of these was 22-year-old Mary Roberts, who had been sentenced by
Glamorgan Court of Quarter Sessions to transportation for life. Her
crime was burglary and stealing clothes. To understand what became of
her and her shipmates it is necessary to know that the year 1812 was a
year in which Britain was at war with America. It was a minor war but
the sea was important in it as the most notable actions of war took place
at sea. The *Emu* was to play a part. Sailing alone, she was approached
by an American privateer, the *Holkar*. The *Holkar* was a formidable
opponent; she was a swift and powerful vessel and carried 150 men.
When confronted, the *Emu's* commander determined to fight, but his
crew, who were better judges of the situation, refused to back him and
the *Emu* surrendered. The Americans boarded their prize and landed
Bissett and the women convicts on the island of St. Vincent in the Cape
Verde islands. Thereafter there is no record of what became of the convict women, but they appear never to have reached Australia.

The voyage of the *Kains* was remarkable in quite a different way. The
Kains, which set sail in July 1830, has gained the reputation of being an
unlucky ship and she certainly had an incredible run of bad luck on this
trip. Again there was just one Welsh woman aboard—Ann, the wife of
Philip Gwyn of Pembrokeshire. Before the *Kains* left Plymouth harbour, she was rammed by another vessel. Just a few days out of port,

the crew mutinied, albeit in a half-hearted way. Then she was accosted by a Spanish pirate vessel but, after contemplation, the Spaniard decided the *Kains* was not worth bothering about and let her sail away. Among other troubles, food ran short and the water ration was drastically reduced. A sailor on board wrote, 'Our bread mouldy and magoty, our beef like oakwood, our water stink and magoty.' The rigging was damaged more than once and as a presentiment of doom to come the sailor diarist records, perhaps fancifully, a sighting of the *Flying Dutchman*. The *Kains* got to New South Wales and did disembark her convicts. She then proceeded to Tasmania but struck a rock en route and was sold off as a wreck.

The short and inexpressibly tragic voyage of the *Amphitrite* stands out in the annals of the convict voyages to Australia. She set sail in September 1833. On board there were 106 female prisoners, 12 of their children, a crew of 16, the captain-owner of the vessel, J. Hunter, and the surgeon, James Forrester and his wife. The vessel was 'proceeding gaily down channel' when she ran into a violent and unexpected gale, accompanied by very heavy seas. Seeing no help for their situation, the captain grounded the vessel on the sands off Boulogne. The tide was low and Hunter dropped anchor. He was waiting for the storm to calm and the tide to rise, thereby floating him off. It was a terrible error of judgement. He did not know local conditions and he did not realise the critical straits in which he had put his ship and all aboard her. Accounts of exactly what happened vary but a French pilot boat sailed out to the *Amphitrite* that night and urged an evacuation. The captain and surgeon refused to disembark the convict women, on the grounds that some might escape. One of the survivors tells the tale that the surgeon's wife was taken off the vessel. He says that the surgeon planned to evacuate the convict women in the long boat, but his wife refused to travel in the same small boat with these women and she stopped her husband from putting the women off. 'Nothing would induce her to sail in the same boat with convicts. Her pride revolted at the idea', said the survivor. At six o'clock that night the *Amphitrite* was three quarters of a mile outside Boulogne harbour and she stood in the greatest peril. A local sailor, who saw that the tragedy was inevitable, actually swam out in the storm and urged the crew to throw out a line . . . but the captain prevented this and the exhausted Frenchman swam back ashore. It is said that that night, the captain and crew, oblivious of the danger, sat down to supper. As for the women and children, it is uncertain whether they were still battened down below or if they had rushed on deck. Their cries are said to have reached the shore. At eleven o'clock that night a mountainous sea struck and immediately the *Amphitrite* broke in two and was smashed to smithereens in seconds. Only three seamen survived and 134 people, mainly convict women, were drowned.

On board the *Amphitrite*, the first convict ship to be lost on the outward run, was a solitary Welsh woman. She was Ann Lewis, a single girl from Dolgellau, and she had been tried a few months earlier at Merioneth Quarter Sessions. She had stolen three hats, one shawl and an umbrella from a shopkeeper. Three other women were tried with her for complicity. One was acquitted but the other two, who were both sentenced to transportation, never actually sailed. Incidentally the *Amphitrite* was the only convict ship which left London during the time Elizabeth Fry was visiting the convict vessels, which she did not visit.

Finally, the *Duchess of Northumberland* deserves a mention as the very last convict vessel to carry women to Tasmania. On board were nine Welsh women, who form the final contingent of Welsh female transportees to sail to Australia. From the sailing of the First Fleet to the voyage of the *Duchess of Northumberland* there were Welsh women aboard the convict transports. It now remains to see what happened to them in the penal colonies.

Chapter 7

THE WELSH CONVICT WOMEN
IN AUSTRALIA

The hovels that we're living in are built of mud and clay,
With rotten straw for bedding, and to that we daren't say nay.
They fence us in with raging fire, and we slumber as we can,
But it keeps away the wolves and tigers upon Van Diemen's Land.

Van Diemen's Land

THE convict ships, which carried women, sailed to one of two destinations, New South Wales or Van Diemen's Land. Convicts were sent via notorious Botany Bay or Port Jackson to New South Wales between 1787 and 1840. During that period 12,460 convict women arrived in New South Wales. Van Diemen's Land, or Tasmania as it is now called, became a penal settlement a little later: male convicts were first sent there in 1812 and by the 1820s female convicts too were being dispatched there. As regards the women, it would appear that for a time, a form of selection operated, and that the worst cases were sent to Van Diemen's Land in the 1820s. This impression is created because a higher proportion of previous offenders was sent to Van Diemen's Land than to New South Wales, and this view is also supported by the fact that a larger number of Scottish women, known as the worst behaved prisoners, were sent to the southern colony. After 1840, when New South Wales was closed down as a prison colony, all women were sent to Van Diemen's Land. The total number sent there was almost exactly the same as to New South Wales, i.e. 12,500. Most of those sent to Tasmania, however, arrived after 1840 and prior to that date only about 3,500 women had been sent there.

The penal system in operation in Australia was very different from the system in the homeland. In Australia convicts were not immediately placed behind bars, because Australia *was* the prison. The *continent* was one vast prison, from which there could be no escape. One needs to see how the system of transportation operated in the colonies and then to look specifically at the Welsh convict women against their new background. I want to concentrate first on New South Wales and then to turn to Van Diemen's Land.

It is an amazing fact that the British government transported the convict women 15,000 miles and when they arrived it had made no provision for them. When the First Fleet sailed into the harbour of Port Jackson, the women could not be disembarked because there was no shelter for them. After that very long voyage they were kept aboard nearly another week, while rudimentary huts were built for them. The British government really abandoned the women and it becomes increasingly obvious that the women were shipped to the colony simply as objects of sexual gratification for the men. Having brought them there, the government simply let them get on with it. With no accommodation provided, the women had no choice. They sold their bodies for a bed and a roof over their heads. The appalling fact is, that a time lapse of about thirty years was allowed to pass before anyone took notice of these abandoned women!

In 1820, thirty-three years after the First Fleet had sailed, Elizabeth Fry railed against the waste of time and money spent in trying to reform these women in England, if they were just to be shunted off to Australia and dumped there as harlots. She spoke of the female convicts as 'without shelter, without resource and without protection', on their arrival in the land of their exile. All that the women received from the authorities was a daily dole out of rations and, as Elizabeth Fry clearly stated, they had nothing of the other basic necessities of life. 'Rations or a small allowance of provision sufficient to maintain life, they certainly had allotted to them daily, but a place to sleep in or the means to obtain one, or the necessary clothing for themselves and when mothers, for their children, they were absolutely without.' Mrs. Fry went as far as to say that to go to the prisons and convict-transports and to preach morality to these women, knowing full well the situation they were going to, was an act of cruelty. To inculcate morality and demand standards, which could not possibly be met by the women was, she believed, merely aggravating their misery. Elizabeth Fry drew much of her information from her informant in New South Wales, the Rev. Samuel Marsden. Writing to her in 1819, he said that he had been working for twenty years in New South Wales to obtain some relief for the convict women, but so far he had had no success. He had already petitioned the Archbishop of Canterbury, the Colonial Office and Members of Parliament about the miserable situation of the convict women and he had been given many glib assurances, but no action had followed on their words. He had been assured as early as 1810 that a barracks would be built to house the convict women but now, years later, they were still waiting. He had also approached the current governor of New South Wales, Lachlan MacQuarie, and so disappointed was Marsden with MacQuarie's unhelpfulness that he widely publicised his letter to the governor. In it he said, 'For the last five and twenty years many of the

Sydney from the west side of the Cove, 1806

Australian Information Service, London

convict women have been driven to vice to obtain a loaf of bread or a bed to lie upon. To this day there never has been a place to put the female convicts in, when they land from the ships.' Marsden went on to relate that many distressed women would gladly have given up their dissolute lifestyle if only they had 'a hut to live in without forming improper connections.' Sometimes, Marsden relates, these women were brought before the magistrates in New South Wales for some petty crime and they have frequently made the plea, 'I have no other means of living, I am compelled to give my weekly allowance of provisions for my lodgings and I must starve or live in vice.' The hypocrisy of the government, which placed them in this predicament, charging some women with prostitution is almost beyond belief! Marsden certainly believed the women's statements, for he knew the real situation, but he was at a loss how to answer them. He was perceptive enough to see not only the harm this neglect did to convict women, but also how very damaging it was for the whole moral climate of the new colony. He alleged that male convicts turned to crime in order to support the women. One could argue that the callousness displayed by officialdom was far more ravaging to the moral economy of the country than the male convicts' crimes, which stemmed from concern.

Now, when one sees the abandonment of the women in the colony, one can begin to appreciate why Elizabeth Fry was so anxious that they should be able to earn a little money by patchwork on the ships.

As Anne Summers, in a recent very good book on the position of women in Australia, past and present, succinctly puts it, 'The women's punishment comprised transportation plus enforced whoredom.' We know that when the women arrived, they were distributed like stores to the settlers. Lord Castlereagh wrote from England to MacQuarie in 1809:

> It has been represented to me that upon the arrival of female convicts in New South Wales, the unfortunate females have been given into the possession of such of the inhabitants, free settlers and convicts, indiscriminately, as made a demand for them from the Governor. If a practice so extraordinary and disgraceful has not been abolished, you will by no means suffer it to continue, and I am to desire you will take the proper means for having the female convicts, upon their arrival, kept separate until they can be properly distributed in such a manner as may best encourage attention to industry and character.

This sort of order from so far away had little effect on practice, though thereafter the distribution took place a fraction more circumspectly. But in 1812 a Select Committee on Transportation still affirmed that the convict women 'were indiscriminately given to such of the inhabitants as demanded them and were in general received rather as prostitutes than servants.' Marsden too said that the custom had been for some years for soldiers, settlers and male convicts to actually board the ships to choose their women. He said this no longer happened openly, but the women were very glad to go to these people because they had no friends or accommodation.

The assignment system of giving out women as servants often led to the same end—prostitution. Single men, in theory, were not supposed to be allocated convict women but they seldom went short. Sometimes, even if a woman was in service with a decent and protective family, she was exposed to many dangers from the men in the neighbourhood. This was partly because the general assumption was that if a woman was a convict she was in fact a prostitute, and partly because of the gross imbalance of the sexes in the colonies, as outlined in Chapter 1. Lord Molesworth commented on the position of a woman in this situation and of the trap in which she was caught:

> At times they are excessively ferocious, and the tendency of assignment is to render them still more profligate; they are all of them, with scarcely an exception, drunken and abandoned prostitutes; and even were any of them inclined to be well-conducted, the disproportion of the sexes in the penal colonies is so great, that they are exposed to irresistible temptations: for instance, in a private family, in the interior of either colony, a convict woman, frequently the only one in the service, perhaps in the neighbourhood, is surrounded by a number of depraved characters, to whom she becomes an object of constant pursuit and solicitation; she is generally obliged to select one as a paramour to defend her from the importunities of the rest; she seldom remains long in the same place; she either commits some offence, for which she is returned to the Government; or she becomes pregnant, in which case she is sent to the factory, to be confined at the expense of the Government, at the expiration of the period of confinement or punishment, she is reassigned, and again goes through the same course; such is too generally the career of convict women, even in respectable families.

Comments by contemporaries in Australia, regarding convict women, were almost all condemnatory. The women were all simply dirty whores, for whom no one had a good word. The Chief Justice of Australia, Andrew Amos, loftily denounced the female transportees and affirmed that, besides the offence for which they were transported, 'they almost always add those of intemperance and unchastity.' As regards the latter what choice did they have? James Mudie, before the 1837 inquiry into transportation, said, 'They all smoke and drink and in

133

fact, in plain language, I consider them all prostitutes.' Mudie's and similar damning comments have been shown in Chapter 1 of this book, where I posed the key question were they all damned whores? We have the answer to that question *before they sailed* and while they were living in Wales, and that answer was emphatically 'No'. About half of the Welsh women were not prostitutes in Wales. Now, we can answer that same question about the women *in the colonies* and the answer is unequivocally, 'Yes'. Mudie and the others spoke the truth. They were, 'in plain language', all prostitutes and it was the transportation system which had made them so.

Life in Australia presented the women with no choice. The only means of survival, prostitution, in many cases shortened their lives. Marsden said that many did not live out half their days from 'habits of vice'. It was his unpleasant and tragic duty as chaplain to be present at many harrowing deathbed scenes and he often heard words such as these, uttered by one dying convict woman:

> Sir, you know how I was situated. I did not wish to lead the life I have done. I know and lament my sins but necessity compelled me to do what my conscience condemned. I could not help myself and must have starved if I had not done as I have.

It is important that we do not see these women's 'occupation' as a job like any other. To do so is to ignore the implications it has for the esteem in which women are held in society. This neglect of the convict women has played a damaging role in degrading the status of women in Australian society and in reinforcing in women an abysmal self-image.

If women had no option but to seek a male protector then marriage was their best bet. Some women, realising this, had conveniently forgotten the existence of husbands back home in Wales and listed themselves as widows or single women. Marriage afforded obvious material advantages. Governor MacQuarie had condemned the 'widespread and pernicious' practice of cohabitation and had tried to encourage marriage by stating that a woman, who merely lived with a man, was not eligible to inherit her 'husband's' possessions on his death. Clearly marriage became even more desirable for women. When one thinks of the large surplus male population in Australia, one would expect every single woman to find a husband with ease, but this was not the case. By the late 1820s just over 40% of the women were married in Australia and this figure only rose slowly thereafter. The explanation lies in the men's attitudes to the convict women. The labels of harlot and whore were sticking and now they were true, even in cases where they had not been before. Mr. Bigge, in an early investigation into conditions in the colony, had reported that male convicts often married convict women and free Australian-born girls but things did not operate in reverse. He said:

> The marriage of the native born youths with female convicts is very rare, a circumstance that is attributed to the general disinclination to early marriage that is observable amongst them, and partly to the abandoned and dissolute habits of the female convicts, but chiefly to a sense of pride in the native born youths, approaching contempt for the vices and depravity of the convicts even when manifested in the persons of their own parents.

Pressure was put on Governor MacQuarie to build a female factory or barracks where the women could live, but MacQuarie, known for his concern for male convicts and celebrated for his interest in building projects, was very dilatory in this matter. He did not begin to build the factory until July 1818 and it was not ready until 1821. Before that date, the only official accommodation which existed for women was a single room! Marsden had persuaded an earlier Governor, Philip Gidley King, to build a storey on top of the men's gaol at Paramatta, about half a day's journey by boat from Sydney. This room was designed, somewhat optimistically, to hold sixty but there were rarely less than 200 women there. Commissioner Bigge described it as follows:

> The factory . . . consists of one long room that is immediately above the gaol, having two windows . . . its dimensions . . . are 60 feet by 20, and at one end are store-rooms, where the wool, yarn and cloth are kept. There is one fireplace, at which all the provisions are cooked. The women have no other beds than those they can make from the wool in its dirty state; and they sleep upon it at night . . . No attempt has been made to preserve cleanliness in this room, as the boards had shrunk so much, that when they were washed, the water fell through them into the prison rooms below.

The majority of women could not be accommodated in this makeshift apartment and went into the town, where they stayed with 'any person who was willing to receive them.'

At last, in 1821, the new factory was opened. It was a three-storey stone building designed to accommodate 300 women and it was to perform the dual function of a prison and a place of employment. The new factory was far more reminiscent of a conventional prison with strictly enforced discipline. The inmates were divided into three classes . . . First, Second, Third or Crime Class. The First Class were only very minor offenders or women returned from assignment, perhaps in ill health: the women of the Second Class were also not serious offenders and women could progress from here to the First Class. The Third, or Crime Class, consisted of women who had bad reports on the voyage or

The old gaol at Paramatta with the female factory on the first floor
National Library of Australia

who had been guilty of misconduct in the colony. When one just reads a classification list the impression is that the women were fairly evenly divided between the classes, but this was not the case. A certain Miss A—, who never gives her name but who was a close friend of Elizabeth Fry, visited the Paramatta factory in the 1830s. She gives a beautiful description of the boat journey, the scenery and a marvellous sunset on her way from Sydney to Paramatta. Then she talks about the factory. She said it was large and airy but ill-adapted either as a prison or as a place of refuge. However, it was clean. It is worth noting that at the time of her visit there were 700 inmates, i.e. well over the limit. She tells us that the First Class consisted of only a very few women, some of whom were filled with shame at their condition. The Second Class had in it many mothers with young babies, these women having been dismissed from assigned service on becoming pregnant. The majority of women in the Paramatta Factory, however, were in the Crime Class. Miss A—, overcoming her nerves, entered the Crime Section. There she was appalled by the sight of women—quarrelling, swearing, drinking, singing or just slumped on the ground.

The Paramatta factory was a place of punishment. In 1836 100 cells were built on to the factory for the purpose of solitary confinement. Miss A— was taken around the cells by Marsden and she thought it a very miserable punishment. Although, she said, the cells were clean and dry, 'they were very dark and comfortless indeed and with only a deal board for a bed.' Miss A— secured the release of one woman, who was being kept there indefinitely, because she refused to name another woman who tried to aid her escape: Miss A— was impressed by her loyalty and prevailed upon the authorities to let her out of solitary confinement. It must be admitted that Marsden had done valuable work in publicising the women's plight, even if he was, at least in part, motivated by a desire to show MacQuarie in a bad light; but Marsden was not all goodness and understanding. He had one woman flogged and dragged by a dray through the streets of Paramatta and another he sentenced to two months on bread and water for refusing to work.

The factory was also to provide work for the non-assigned women. Some were engaged in washing, needlework, picking oakum and in weaving, until the loom was removed as an economy measure in 1835. Hard labour there could mean breaking stones for road building. Normally, however, the factory was overcrowded and there was not enough work. Finally, Paramatta factory was unashamedly used as a marriage mart and brothel. Any man, ex-convict or settler, could turn up at the factory to look the women over and take one off as his 'wife'. He simply had a word with the matron (and there were many sharp allegations later made against that lady) and she gave the order for the women to be paraded out. The women 'are turned out, and they all

137

The later female factory at Paramatta from a painting by Augustus Earle
Rex Nan Kivell Collection, National Library of Australia

stand up as you would place so many soldiers, or so many cattle, in fact, in a fair; they are all ranked up . . . The convict goes up and looks at the women, and if he sees a lady that takes his fancy, he makes a motion to her, and she steps to one side; some will not, but stand still, and have no wish to be married, but that is very rare. Then they have, of course, some conversation together and if the lady is not agreeable, or if the convict does not fancy her from her conversation, she steps back and the same ceremony goes on with two or three more.' There are stories of very fastidious men who went through hundreds of women and found not one to their liking, but most were easier to please.

In a place like the factory the women could react in two main ways. They could submit to its rigorous discipline and become subdued creatures, or they could rebel against it and break out riotously. We see evidence of both kinds of behaviour. A visitor there in 1847 said that the women are so strictly kept, 'that I do not well see have they could evince any of their evil spirit . . . The women are not allowed to talk . . . the women are remarkably clean, and neatly dressed. They have their hair closely cut when they first enter the factory . . . They are kept always busy sewing and washing.' They were broken women and they internalised the guilt they were told they should feel for their often petty crime. It is a terribly sad picture of the female transportees. But there is evidence too of the women acting in a far more outgoing manner and giving vent to their anger and turning it outwards. On one occasion at Paramatta 'four or five hundred of the most abandoned women of the Empire' threw everything over the walls of the prison. In a big riot in 1827, started by the Criminal Class, who claimed they were starving, the women broke their way out and plundered the local food shops. Having eaten, most returned to the factory. Somehow this seems a healthier reaction than the docile submission demanded of them. Many children were born in the factories and the mortality rate, especially in Van Diemen's Land, was very high. The children were not kept in the factory with their mothers. They were placed in orphan schools.

But the factory was not the destination of all convicts. Some, with a good report from the ship's surgeon or captain or a pretty face, went straight into assigned service. The women had no choice in this matter, just as a slave would have no say. The master chose her, and if she failed to please him, he sent her back to the factory and got a replacement. Whereas assigned male convicts were always in demand as heavy labourers, there was less call for female servants. Sir Francis Forbes said in 1837, 'generally the applications for them as female servants, are too limited to take them off the hands of government and there is always a large body of them in the factory.' Normally a low opinion was held of these outcast women. Forbes thought they were more nuisance than they were worth. James Mudie, appearing before the 1837 Committee

139

The female orphan school, Paramatta

Rex Nan Kivell Collection, National Library of Australia

of Inquiry, explained, 'if you apply for instance for a dairymaid or housemaid, perhaps you will have a lady sent to you that has been walking the lobby of the theatres: this is your dairymaid.' There was reluctance among many female employers to let the convict women near their children, lest they corrupt them. It is true that a few convict women were charged with being drunk in charge of a child. Some employers were prepared to treat assigned servants quite reasonably and even this aroused resentment among other employers. E. A. Slade, another witness before the 1837 Commission, was appalled to find that female convicts were treated as well as servants in England. 'They have tea', he lamented, 'they have sugar, they have beer, they have rum on washing days.' These were the lucky ones.

The whole system of assignment was wide open to abuse. The authorities occasionally expressed concern about the misuse of female convict servants. We have seen Molesworth's picture of the convict servant in the countryside as a prey for all the men from miles around, and, even within a household, the convict woman would be expected to oblige the master and sons. Respectable newspapers attacked not only masters and their sons for this but also the mothers and daughters, who knew full well what was going on. There seems to have been very little sense of obligation and concern on the part of middle class women for their less fortunate sisters. This is in contrast to Britain and America. There were even extreme cases of abuse of female convicts. Some men had them assigned to them and lived off their immoral earnings.

Assignment was a lottery. A young woman—perhaps one of the Welsh first offenders—could be lucky and be sent to a caring family, or she could be very unlucky and be assigned as the mistress of some old settler. Male convicts, of course, also suffered and many of them worked virtually in slave gangs. A slight complaint from the master or mistress—or a trumped-up accusation—meant a return to the factory and a delay before the woman could apply for a ticket of leave. When Miss A— toured Paramatta she received a large number of complaints from the women, 'that bad masters and cruel mistresses made them worse than they were: that in service they were treated "like dogs" and seldom spoken to without an oath, or treated as devils more than human beings.' Miss A— told of two lovely looking young women who were in Paramatta because they had murdered their former master. They were both repentant for their action, but they kept cryptically insisting that he had deserved it.

A telling indictment of the assignment system is the fact that many women were quite happy to return to the factory. But, on the other hand, failure to complete a year's satisfactory assignment could mean refusal of permission to marry. Many bad employers, if it suited them, would say that the woman's service was unsatisfactory. The government, however, became increasingly less happy with the assignment system and eventually discontinued it. Such was the situation in which the Welsh convict women found themselves. Their fate was to be the factory, assigned service, marriage for some, and hopefully a ticket of leave, which gave them a degree of freedom while still under police supervision. Ultimately they could gain a pardon. Prostitution was, of course, linked with all of these possibilities. It would be interesting to look specifically at some of the Welsh transportees and see what became of them. To a certain extent it is possible to do this for the women in New South Wales—though not with the wealth of detail I have found for Tasmania.

The authorities in New South Wales kept records, rather like census returns, of convicts who entered the colony and recorded against their name what had become of them. It also noted their date of arrival and we see at a glance that the women were in the colony many, many years after the expiration of the original sentence of transportation. The name of the ship on which they sailed was also entered since each convict was always known and spoken of by her own name and the name of her ship. Mary Davies would no longer be plain Mary Davies but Mary Davies—*Lady Juliana*.

These records are not absolutely reliable and complete. A Welsh woman put down as dead in 1819 pops up alive and married in Sydney in 1820! But they give us a fair indication of the women's fate. In the Nominal Alphabetical Return for Female Convicts in 1820, I have found the names of thirty-eight women sentenced in Wales. If we break this number down according to what became of them we see the following:

Married	14
Widows	1
Single	7
Domestic Service	8
Factory	1
Ticket of Leave	3
Left the Colony	3
Hospital	1
Total:	38

The married women were nearly all living in the growing town of Sydney with their husbands. All the single women lived there and, with no other designation, we can assume they were prostitutes. Those in domestic service were spread around the colony and one is designated as a country servant. Another woman was given as an assigned servant to

Circular quay, Sydney, in 1870
Australian Information Service, London

her husband. Only one Welsh woman was in the factory. This is not surprising in 1820, because the new factory had not yet been built and the factory was still the single upstairs room. Actually the previous year, 1819, had seen three Welsh women in that squalid room and the earlier years may well have seen more. In the 1820 list we see that many women had been in New South Wales for over twenty years, even though they were transported for seven years. They had no chance of getting far. The three who had left the colony most probably only went to Van Diemen's Land.

In some ways the Welsh girls were well equipped to play a useful role in frontier life. They were country girls and they possessed the right skills for life in a rural community. Margaret Griffiths—*Northampton*, from St. Mellons, Monmouthshire, worked as a country servant in the hinterland. Mary Lewis—*Nile* from rural Merionethshire was tried in 1793: in 1819 we hear of her still working as a settler's wife in the outback.

It is not part of my aim here to trace the subsequent fortunes of the male convicts and I mention them only in contrast with the women. Some of these floundered and suffered very hard fates, but many had exciting prospects and did far better than they could ever have hoped to have done in Wales. A quick glance at the records for men shows them being granted land and becoming settlers, others becoming businessmen and shopkeepers and yet others becoming police constables and even lawyers! This is the bright side of the transportation picture, but it was not shared by women. The one or two women who triumphed, despite all the odds, are so exceptional that they are famous in Australian history.

Turning to the southern colony, where most women were later sent, we see a very similar situation. On the island prison of Tasmania there were two major female factories, the Cascades factory at Hobart and the other at Launceston. Cascades was an old distillery before it was converted into a female factory. A contemporary description of it chills the bones.

> Situated in a morass, surrounded by lofty hills, the sun's rays bringing with them health and cheerfulness do not penetrate into the yards of that miserable prison for a great portion of the entire year. The capacity of the building is so unequal to the number of the wretched inmates, that their working rooms resemble the hold of a slave-ship . . . So foetid, so wholly unfitting for the human being is the atmosphere after the night's halations, that if we are correctly informed, the turnkeys when they open the doors in the mornings, make their escape from the passages with the utmost expedition to escape semi-suffocation.

144

Prisoners at Cascades were divided into three classes, as at Paramatta, and only from the First Class could women be assigned. Punishments administered there were vicious. For many years a refined piece of cruelty was inflicted: the women wore heavy iron collars, weighing about 14-15 pounds, and with a long spike sticking out of each side, this giving the women 'the appearance of horned cattle.' At this factory there were also dark and damp cells for solitary confinement and in the 1830s a treadmill was introduced there. (New South Wales had had one for ten years). This barbaric instrument of torture, used a great deal in British prisons, consisted of a large 'revolving cylinder to which was fastened a circular frame. This was fitted with steps around the circumference, rather like the paddle wheel of an early steamship. The drum could either be filled with stones or connected to a flour mill or pump. When the convict put his foot on to a step, the drum revolved, and to avoid falling off he had to keep on mounting continuously to the next step above. This process continued for whatever number of hours each day were thought appropriate by the authorities.' The treadmill would be operated for many hours at a stretch. It was built to accommodate the height and stronger physiques of men. On women it had a most dreadful effect. It produced a terrible pain in the loins, haemorrhaging and miscarriages. There was, let it be known, one in use in Cardiff gaol.

The factory, like in Paramatta, was also a maternity hospital and it is as such that Cascades has drawn considerable criticism. This factory had an incredibly high infant mortality rate. Babies there were undernourished and their mothers were punished for becoming pregnant. The daily ration for an adult woman was:

Bread	1 lb.
Meat	8 oz.
Potatoes	8 oz.
or	
Cabbage	1 lb.
Sugar	1 oz.
Roasted Wheat	1 oz.
Salt	½ oz.

Crime class women did not receive the roasted wheat and sugar (used to make a hot coffee-like drink) and they were given 2 ozs. of oatmeal instead. Nor were the hours of serving food very satisfactory. In one ward there was nothing to eat from midday until 8.00 a.m. the next. The babies were fed on milk, bread and sugar and when they became ill, as they frequently did on the low protein diet, they were put on to wine and sago!

Conditions were very cramped at Cascades and it has been compared with the hold of a slave ship. There was a constant intake of women returned from assignment for misconduct or for becoming pregnant. The harsher punishments have already been mentioned. The more routine punishment was 'at the wash tub' and the unpopular cropping off of hair. Whilst in the factory the women wore a uniform of 'white mob caps and a dress of grey duffle', an outfit, as one aristocratic visitor remarked, 'which was unbecoming to the person, however becoming to the station of the wearer.' The laundrywork was very heavy whilst the needlework was a mixture of very fine sewing and the manufacture of the coarse prison dresses. A glimpse into the work areas is afforded us by the visitor who observed:

> One of the great yards of the factory was devoted to laundress work. Squads of women were up to their elbows in suds—carrying on the cruel process of wringing—or displaying their thick ankles as they spread the linen over the drying lines. The townsfolk may have their washing done here at 1s. 6d. per dozen, the money going towards the expenses of the institution. I was pained to see so many young creatures in this yard—delinquents in the earliest teens; debauched ere the pith had hardened in their little bones. We had next a glimpse of a room full of sempstresses, most of them employed on fine work. It was not impossible, the matron stated, that some of the elaborate shirt-fronts we should see at the Government-house ball this evening had been worked in this, and washed and 'got up' in the last ward. A rougher fabric done by the less skilled prisoners is a coarse kind of woollen tweed, only used for prison dresses.

Under the regime at Cascades some women were very subdued, but other ebullient spirits showed what they thought of the place and its controllers. There was a group in Cascades called the 'Flash Mob', who just used the factory when they liked and went off to taverns when they pleased. According to the *Colonial Times* newspaper in 1840, a favourite resort of the Flash Mob on a Sunday afternoon was the military barracks. One incident at the factory shows the humour of some of the women. One day the factory was being visited by an eminent party, the Governor, Sir John Franklin, and his wife Lady Jane, an aide-de-camp and several ladies. Accompanying them around was the very pompous clergyman, the Reverend Bedford. The assembled women listened with good grace as first Sir John and then his wife addressed them. Then came the Reverend Bedford's turn to speak. The women knew the reverend gentleman for what he was, a bore and a hypocrite, who loved food and bottles of port far more than the scriptures. They had to put up with his wordy and boring sermons as a rule,

Female House of Correction, Tasmania
State Library of Tasmania

but that day they had had enough. As Bedford rose to preach, there was a loud outbreak of coughing. The warders ordered silence and so the women obeyed. As one, they turned around, raised their itchy prison dresses and 'smacked their posteriors with a loud report.' The Reverend Bedford had his come-uppance. The governor was shocked but the aide-de-camp and the visiting ladies burst out laughing.

In studying the convict women in Tasmania, one change in the transportation system must be noted. Much criticism had led to the official discontinuation of the assignment system and in its place Lord Stanley, Secretary of State for the Colonies, introduced the probation system. This greatly altered the character of transportation for men but really it did not mean a very great change for women. The new plan was as follows: the women were to spend six months in a new penitentiary which was to be built, and in the meantime a ship, the man-of-war *Anson* was to act as a temporary prison. After this six-month stint, the women were to go to employment where they would receive a small wage. The payment of wages was a good innovation and a necessary one. The work was exactly the same as under the assignment system, i.e. domestic service. The period of employment whilst on probation was divided into three stages, each paid better than the last. Such was the imaginative scheme, but it did not work out. The penitentiary was not built and the women were either aboard the *Anson*, in the factory or working as domestics. Economic difficulties and a depression in the 1840s meant a shortage of jobs. However, the women progressed towards tickets of leave and pardons. On average they obtained the tickets about four to five years after arriving in Tasmania.

Assiduous record keeping in Tasmania enables us to trace the Welsh convict women on the island. I have followed up the subsequent lives of 100 Welsh women there. Of that 100, only seven got into serious trouble and appeared before the superior courts. A further seventy-three had some slight blemish on their conduct sheets, but despite the fact that these incidents were punished we cannot call them crimes. Misconduct included insolence to employers, drunkenness, staying out too late, being in a town without a pass, slovenly work or malingering. A decision whether to report these usually lay with the employer. Finally, twenty of the Welsh women had no black mark at all on their record sheets and very quickly won tickets of leave.

In order to give a picture of the lives of the Welsh women in Van Diemen's Land, it is most useful to turn to stories of individual women. I have chosen a few women as examples since I believe them to be typical.

Among that very small group of Welsh women who got into serious trouble in Van Diemen's Land, was Mary Cecil, a freckled-faced country servant originally transported by order of Monmouth Assizes for stealing three sovereigns from a man. She had been committed before and we know that she had been on the town six years, from the age of 23. In Tasmania she had married but she had not abandoned her old ways. She appeared before the Superior Court at Hobart charged with assaulting a certain Mr. Chapman and robbing him of £7. She was already in the final year of her original ten year sentence, so the court sentenced her to a new term of fifteen years. This is not so harsh as it sounds and the court only stipulated she should serve two years probation. By 1860, sixteen years after her trial at Monmouth, she had won her ticket of leave, but this was to be revoked the following year because she was absent and therefore deemed to have absconded. There is no further record of Mary Cecil.

Ann Evans, transported from Glamorgan in January 1833 for stealing cheese, had previous offences in Wales and the reputation of a thief. In Tasmania she was regularly returned from service and spent several periods in solitary confinement and on bread and water. For her first colonial offence of larceny, she escaped with a stint at the factory, but when she stole money in 1838 the court extended her existing sentence from seven to eight years transportation. In fact she received a certificate of freedom, nine years after her original sentence. Elizabeth Morgan, tried in the same Welsh county for stealing a cooking pan, had a long criminal record in Wales. She committed petty offences in Tasmania including being out after hours, for which she served fourteen days at the washtub, and the use of abusive language at the race track, for which she was reprimanded. She also committed a more serious offence, i.e. theft and for this she was brought before the Court of Quarter Sessions in 1845 and was punished by a period of confinement.

Turning away from the colonial offenders, we find that the majority of women were guilty, at one time or another, of some sort of misconduct or objectionable behaviour. It is their lives, I think, which give us the most representative insight into women's lives in the colony.

Elizabeth Thomas was sent to Tasmania in the early days. Tried in Beaumaris in March 1823, she sailed on the *Brothers* to Tasmania and arrived the next year. She was a first offender and she had stolen worn clothing. She had quarrelled with her parents and gone off to live with her young man. They had a child but the baby had died in prison before she sailed. On arrival in Tasmania, she was put in the factory, but she was in trouble for attempting to escape. She literally broke her way out and was charged with 'breaking a hole in the wall of the female factory on the night on December 5th instant and escaping thereby.' She remained at large for some time but was later apprehended and returned to the factory. Her punishments were very harsh. Firstly her hair was

149

to be cut off, then she was put in a cell on bread and water and finally she was ordered to wear the infamous pronged iron collar for seven days.

Ruth Roberts of Bala, Merionethshire, a 41-year-old laundress, travelled out to Tasmania aboard the *Cadet*, 1847-8, and was well behaved on the voyage. During her Tasmanian sojourn, she conducted herself well. Her only offence appears to have taken place on the hulk *Anson*. There she was charged with 'trafficing in disposing of her wedding ring.' She probably needed the money. She was punished for this by a month's extra probation. Her normal good behaviour was, however, rewarded and by 1851 she had a ticket of leave and two years later a pardon.

Elizabeth Hughson, aged 22 on arrival, and a pale, dark haired, servant girl from Brecon, had been convicted for shoplifting. She had a previous offence, stealing a leg of mutton, and she is said to have kept very bad company in Brecon. Once in Tasmania, where she arrived in 1829, she spent the next seven years in and out of minor trouble. She was quickly assigned out as a servant but soon sent back for drunkenness and going absent without leave: for this she was put in the Crime Class at Cascades. On later assignments she accused her master of turning another female servant against her. This meant another return to confinement and the recommendation that she should not be assigned anywhere near Hobart town. On her next venture into domestic service, Elizabeth was in trouble again. This time she was caught in a compromising position with a soldier in the master's stable and for this she got three months hard labour. Her career continued in this vein until she obtained a ticket of leave.

Ann Lee was a native of Shropshire and she came from a village near Shrewsbury. She was transported from Monmouthshire for assault with intent to rob but had no previous offences. She was a tough customer; her behaviour in gaol was bad. She was transported to Tasmania early on, at the time when most refractory women were sent there. She arrived in 1830 on the *Eliza*. In April 1830 she was insolent to that unpopular man, the Reverend Bedford, and he had her placed in a cell on bread and water for a week. She was available for assignment as long as it was far away in the interior. But her new mistress complained about her general insolence and the fact that she was 'continually using blasphemous expressions and profane oaths.' Ann was then sent to George Town for further confinement and she spent the next few years between domestic service and imprisonment.

On the same day that Ann Lee had been sentenced to transportation in Monmouthshire, another young woman received the same sentence there. She was Ann Pike and she sailed with Ann Lee on the *Eliza*. Her colonial record contained the now familiar insolence and disrespectful conduct. She was also returned to the prison on one occasion for doing a paid job: assigned servants were not allowed to work for money.

Hannah Roberts, the young Flintshire girl, who in league with her lover, poisoned her husband with arsenic, was still only twenty when she arrived in Tasmania on the *Emma Eugenia* in 1844. Although the court recognised that she was of a giddy disposition, her status in Wales was given as poor but respectable. Men seem to have been Hannah's passion and the cause of her downfall. In 1846 she had remarried in Van Diemen's Land, was apparently living quietly, but a few years later she came off the rails again. In 1850 she was found out after hours in a public house and for this she was sentenced to a month's hard labour. She was forbidden to work in Hobart itself. Her new husband, John Cadby, disappeared somewhere along the line and in 1852 Hannah was living with another man, whom she falsely represented as her husband. This was an offence and she had to serve a month's hard labour for it. Men continued to figure in Hannah's life. She was found a little later with a 'male prisoner of the crown' concealed in her bedroom for an improper purpose, as the record says. This earned her three days in the cells but, undeterred, she repeated the offence within the month and this time had to serve three months hard labour. Nevertheless, despite this unpromising period she was awarded a ticket of leave in 1854, ten years after her arrival. Yet Hannah was on the downward path. There followed a whole series of charges involving drink and men. If Hannah's crime was just a crime of passion and if as a young girl she had been led astray by her lover, she had to pay dearly for it, living a wretched and drunken life 15,000 miles from home.

Another Hannah, Hannah Evans, born in Carmarthen but working in Glamorgan, was transported for buying stolen goods. Apparently a first offender, she was tried with her husband, whom she left behind in the penitentiary. She was aged 40 and she had four children. She was a good servant, but one or two minor incidents led to a six-week spell at the wash-tub and to assignment in the interior. Her only later 'crime' was gossipping in the streets, and this offence was actually recorded on her colonial record.

There was a whole range of other reportable and punishable offences. Others for which Welsh women were punished included abusing a police constable, keeping a disorderly house, being found in a brothel, misappropriating a towel and repairing her stays with it, breaking glass in her mistress's windows, being in a public house with a sailor and sheltering a female absconder. Some incidents were rather more serious such as smashing up her husband's furniture and threatening him with a knife. Cases of absconding were treated seriously. A reward of £1 was offered for the capture of Maria Meyrick of Glamorgan and in such cases the sentence of transportation was sometimes extended.

On the other hand, we must remember that 20% of Welsh convict women had an absolutely clean sheet. Many of these were first offenders. Mary Jones, the young country girl from Caernarvonshire who had killed her illegitimate child, was never in any trouble. A dairy maid at home, she was assigned to a farm in Van Diemen's Land. It is, however, a surprising fact that not all of this 20% were first offenders. Some were quite frequent offenders at home but they settled down in Australia and may even have been better off.

Of the hundred Welsh women in Tasmania whose lives I have traced, sixty said they were single and seventeen made a claim to widowhood. In theory, all these were eligible to marry. In fact, I have found that only twenty-two of them did marry and one suspects that exactly the same reluctance to marry convict women existed among the men there, as did in New South Wales. Illegitimate children were common in the penal colonies. At least six, and very likely more, of the Welsh convict women in Tasmania bore illegitimate children. Of the six babies, two died in infancy. Elizabeth Williams, a tiny nursery maid from 'Murtagh Tidwell', as the Tasmanian record reads, was delivered of an illegitimate child in the factory on 10 November, 1850. The baby girl, named Selina, died in February 1852 after Elizabeth had in fact married the master to whom she was assigned. Mary Holehouse of Monmouthshire who took one of her illegitimate children with her on board the *Tory* in 1845, had another baby in January 1847 at the Hobart factory, but the child died in September of that year. These deaths could well have been the result of the undernourishment of babies in the Hobart factory, which caused such a storm of criticism at the time against the matron, Mrs. Hutchinson. She herself had twelve children, six of whom died in infancy.

Finally, the case of Elizabeth Morris, tried at Presteigne is interesting. She had been convicted before for stealing apples and she was transported for stealing clothes. She had a young baby whom she brought with her on the *Sea Queen* in 1846. By 1850 she had a ticket of leave and applied for her family to join her. This sometimes happened with convict men, but it is the only case of a woman doing this which I have come across. It is not known if they did come, but if they did sail out, it would have meant the arrival of her mother, Margaret Williams, her brothers, William and John, sisters Ann and Mary, and maybe even Thomas Watkins 'the father of my child'.

Transportation to New South Wales had ceased in 1840 and by the later part of the decade opposition to transportation among the free settlers was growing in Tasmania too. Between 1846 and 1848 transportation was suspended. It was resumed but only for a few years and 1852 saw the departure from England of the last convict ship carrying women.

These convict women had been transported many thousands of miles from home, usually for petty offences, and one in three had no previous convictions. Some had been on the streets at home, yet now they were all forced into prostitution. Their chances of returning home to Wales were virtually non-existent. Condemned to exile, a very hard life lay before most of them. Their hopes lay with the next generation, with 'the currency' as their children were called.

*　　*　　*　　*

As one reads history . . . one is absolutely sickened not by the crimes the wicked have committed, but by the punishments the good have inflicted

Oscar Wilde

APPENDIX

Abbreviations of Court Names

Ass. = Assizes
QS = Quarter Sessions
GS = Great Sessions

Female Transportees—Anglesey

Name	Court	Date of Trial	Ship	Destination	Sentence
Mary Thomas (al. Lewis)	GS	March 1823	Brothers	V.D.L.	7 years
Ann Williams (al. Edwards)	Ass.	March 1842	Garland Grove	V.D.L.	10 ”
Elizabeth Williams	QS	January 1843	Emma Eugenia	V.D.L.	7 ”
Mary Owen (al. Williams)	QS	January 1849	St. Vincent	V.D.L.	7 ”
Jessie White	QS	January 1850	Emma Eugenia	V.D.L.	10 ”
Ellen Davies	Ass.	July 1850	Aurora	V.D.L.	7 ”

Female Transportees—Breconshire

Name	Court	Date of Trial	Ship	Destination	Sentence
Catherine Williams	GS	April 1789	?	N.S.W.	7 years
Ann Smith	GS	March 1802	Experiment	N.S.W.	7 ”
Margaret Jones	GS	April 1803	”	N.S.W.	Life
Elizabeth Woods	GS	August 1804	William Pitt	N.S.W.	7 years
Mary David (al. Philips)	GS	April 1808	Indispensible	N.S.W.	7 ”
Ann Morgan	GS	August 1816	Friendship	N.S.W.	7 ”
Ann Pugh	GS	September 1819	Morley	N.S.W. or V.D.L.	Life
Elizabeth Hughson	QS	January 1829	Lady of the Lake	V.D.L.	7 years
Ann Griffiths	QS	March 1832	Francis Charlotte	V.D.L.	7 ”
Eliza Williams	QS	October 1832	Jane	V.D.L.	7 ”
Sarah Waters	QS	October 1832	”	V.D.L.	7 ”
Jane Price (al. Margaret Lewis)	QS	March 1833	William Bryan	V.D.L.	7 ”
Typhena Morgan (al. Prothero)	Ass.	July 1833	Numa	N.S.W.	7 ”
Maria Barker (al. Bell al. Jackson)	QS	July 1834	New Grove	V.D.L.	7 ”

Name	Court	Date of Trial	Ship	Destination	Sentence
Mary Morgan (al. Pearce)	Ass.	July 1834	,,	V.D.L.	7 ,,
Mary Owens	QS	October 1838	Hindostan	V.D.L.	7 ,,
Catherine Lewis	QS	October 1844	Tory	V.D.L.	7 ,,
Mary Atkins	Ass.	March 1845	Lloyds	V.D.L.	10 ,,
Hannah Dainty (al. Williams)	QS	October 1845	Emma Eugenia	V.D.L.	7 ,,
Ann Williams (al. Mary Gilbert)	QS	July 1849	St. Vincent	V.D.L.	7 ,,

Female Transportees—Cardiganshire

Name	Court	Date of Trial	Ship	Destination	Sentence
Eleanor James	GS	September 1822	Brothers	V.D.L.	7 years

Female Transportees—Caernarvonshire

Name	Court	Date of Trial	Ship	Destination	Sentence
Ann Jones (al. Parry)	GS	March 1812	Wanstead	N.S.W.	7 years
Mary Williams	GS	Summer 1817	Maria	N.S.W.	Life
Mary Roberts	GS	Summer 1817	,,	N.S.W.	Life
Jane Griffiths	GS	April 1824	Henry	V.D.L.	7 years
Charlotte Davies	GS	August 1824	,,	V.D.L.	7 ,,
Eleanor Williams	GS	March 1825	Midas	N.S.W. or V.D.L.	7 ,,
Elizabeth Lloyd (al. Owen)	GS	March 1826	Princess Charlotte	N.S.W.	Life
Catherine Jones	GS	April 1827	Sovereign	V.D.L.	Life
Elizabeth Jones	GS	April 1827	,,	V.D.L.	Life
Mary Griffith	Ass.	March 1836	Westmoreland	V.D.L.	Life
Amelia Evans	Ass.	March 1836	,,	V.D.L.	Life
Elizabeth Rowlands	Ass.	March 1839	Mary Ann	N.S.W.	7 years
Mary Smith	Ass.	July 1844	Tory	V.D.L.	10 ,,
Margaret Presdee	QS	October 1844	,,	V.D.L.	7 ,,
Elizabeth Thomas	QS	January 1847	Cadet	V.D.L.	10 ,,
Mary Jones	Ass.	July 1850	Aurora	V.D.L.	Life

Female Transportees—Carmarthenshire

Name	Court	Date of Trial	Ship	Destination	Sentence
Rachel Davies	GS	August 1791	Royal Admiral	N.S.W.	7 years
Elizabeth Davies	GS	January 1792	Kitty	N.S.W.	Life
Hannah Williams	GS	August 1800	Nile	N.S.W.	7 years
Ann Lloyd	GS	April 1801	Experiment	N.S.W.	Life

Name	Court	Date of Trial	Ship	Destination	Sentence
Martha Daniel (al. David)	GS	April 1801	,,	N.S.W.	Life
Sarah Smith	GS	August 1802	,,	N.S.W.	7 years
Rachel Griffiths	GS	August 1803	,,	N.S.W.	7 years
Margaret Daniel	Ass.	April 1813	Broxbournebury	N.S.W.	7 ,,
Lucy Cole (al. Loveday)	GS	September 1828	Lucy Davidson	N.S.W.	7 ,,
Rebecca Lloyd	GS	April 1829	,, ,,	N.S.W.	Life
Mary Lewis	QS	July 1829	Eliza	V.D.L.	7 years
Charlotte Williams	Ass.	July 1831	Frances Charlotte	V.D.L.	14 ,,
Mary Lewis	Ass.	March 1834	George Hibbart	N.S.W.	Life
Sarah Gunter	Ass.	July 1834	New Grove	V.D.L.	7 years
Elizabeth Burnett	QS	February 1837	Henry Wellesley	N.S.W.	7 ,,
Sarah James	Ass.	March 1837	,, ,,	N.S.W.	7 ,,
Mary Connick	Ass.	March 1837	,, ,,	N.S.W.	7 ,,
Eleanor Williams	Ass.	March 1841	Emma Eugenia	V.D.L.	15 ,,
Mary Williams (al. Presley)	QS	January 1842	Royal Admiral	V.D.L.	7 ,,
Mary Davies	QS	October 1843	Tasmania	V.D.L.	7 ,,
Ann Matthews	Ass.	May 1849	St. Vincent	V.D.L.	10 ,,
Mary Blake	QS	March 1852	Duchess of Northumberland	V.D.L.	7 ,,

Female Transportees—Denbighshire

Name	Court	Date of Trial	Ship	Destination	Sentence
Sarah Evans	QS	July 1786	Neptune	N.S.W.	7 years
Grace Jones	QS	July 1786	,,	N.S.W.	7 ,,
Margaret Jones	QS	January 1793	Indispensible	N.S.W.	7 ,,
Ann Jones	QS	January 1793	,,	N.S.W.	7 ,,
Ann Hughes (al. wife of David Roberts)	QS	October 1793	,,	N.S.W.	7 ,,
Elizabeth Edwards	QS	January 1795	,,	N.S.W.	7 ,,
Catherine Owens	GS	August 1801	Glatton	N.S.W.	7 ,,
Margaret Jones	GS	April 1817	Friendship	N.S.W.	7 ,,
Ann Jemima Parry	GS	August 1822	Mary	N.S.W. or V.D.L.	7 ,,
Alice Lunt	GS	March 1824	Henry	V.D.L.	Life
Eleanor Owens	GS	March 1824	,,	V.D.L.	Life
Ann Miles	GS	July 1826	Persia	V.D.L.	14 years
Ellen Roberts	GS	July 1826	,,	V.D.L.	14 ,,
Ellen Roberts	GS	April 1827	Harmony	V.D.L.	14 ,,
Jane Edwards	GS	March 1828	,,	V.D.L.	14 ,,
Ann Jones	?	October 1830	America	V.D.L.	7 ,,
Ellin Parry	QS	April 1832	Fanny	N.S.W.	7 ,,

Name	Court	Date of Trial	Ship	Destination	Sentence
Catherine Jones	Ass.	August 1836	*Platina*	V.D.L.	14 "
Ann Capper	QS	January 1837	*Henry Wellesley*	N.S.W.	7 "
Ann (Hannah) Evans	QS	January 1839	*Surrey*	N.S.W.	7 "
Eliz. Williams	Ass.	July 1838	*Garland Grove*	V.D.L.	Life
Ellen Davies	Ass.	July 1842	" "	V.D.L.	10 years
Bridget Harris	QS	December 1844	*Tory*	V.D.L.	7 "
Mary Tracey	QS	January 1847	*Elizabeth & Henry*	V.D.L.	7 "
Elizabeth Williams	QS (?)	March 1850	*Emma Eugenia*	V.D.L.	7 "
Mary Jones	QS	July 1850	*Aurora*	V.D.L.	7 "
Martha Priddin	QS	October 1850	"	V.D.L.	7 "
Susannah Friday (Foundling— al. Mary S. Williams)	QS	March 1852	*Duchess of Northumberland*	V.D.L.	7 "

Female Transportees—Flintshire

Name	Court	Date of Trial	Ship	Destination	Sentence
Frances Williams	—	1783	*Prince of Wales*	N.S.W.	7 years
Elinor Richards	Ass.	February 1837	*Henry Wellesley*	N.S.W.	7 "
Hannah Roberts	Ass.	July 1842	*Emma Eugenia*	V.D.L.	Life
Catherine Magrath	QS	October 1842	" "	V.D.L.	10 years
Catherine Baker	QS	March 1848	*Cadet*	V.D.L.	10 "

Female Transportees—Glamorgan

Name	Court	Date of Trial	Ship	Destination	Sentence
Mary Watkins	QS	April 1786	*Friendship*	N.S.W.	7 years
Sarah Burt (al. Jenny Phillip)	GS	September 1791	*Royal Admiral*	N.S.W.	Life
Mary Jenkins	QS	January 1792	" "	N.S.W.	7 years
Margaret Thomas Beynon	GS	March 1797	*Nile*	N.S.W.	Life
Ann David	GS	March 1798	"	N.S.W.	Life
Sarah Richards	GS	March 1796	"	N.S.W.	7 years
Margaret Davies (al. Mary ux J. Jones)	GS	August 1801	*Glatton*	N.S.W.	7 "
Alice Williams	GS	August 1802	*Experiment*	N.S.W.	7 "
Mary James	GS	August 1808	*Canada*	N.S.W.	7 "
Ann Thomas	GS	March 1809	"	N.S.W.	Life
Mary Roberts (age 22)	QS	March 1812	*Emu*	N.S.W.	Life
Margaret Griffith	GS	April 1814	*Northampton*	N.S.W.	7 years
Ann Thomas	GS	April 1828	*Competitor*	N.S.W.	7 "
Margaret Ellis	QS	April 1828	"	N.S.W.	7 "

158

Name	Court	Date of Trial	Ship	Destination	Sentence
Martha Davies	QS	April 1828	,,	N.S.W.	7 ,,
Mary Willson	QS	July 1829	Roslin Castle	N.S.W.	7 ,,
Elizabeth Jones	QS	October 1829	,, ,,	N.S.W.	7 ,,
Anne Gill	QS	October 1829	,, ,,	N.S.W.	7 ,,
Elizabeth Morgan	QS	January 1830	America	V.D.L.	7 ,,
Lucretia Davies	Ass.	July 1831	Pyramus	N.S.W.	Life
Mary Cornic	Ass.	July 1831	,,	N.S.W.	Life
Mary Morris	QS	January 1833	Buffalo	N.S.W.	7 years
Anne Tratten	Ass.	February 1833	,,	N.S.W.	7 ,,
Hannah Evans	Ass.	February 1833	William Bryon	V.D.L.	7 ,,
Anne Evans	QS	January 1833	Edward	V.D.L.	7 ,,
Rachel Evans	QS	October 1833	,,	V.D.L.	7 ,,
Mary Noble	QS	December 1833	,,	V.D.L.	14 ,,
Margaret Edwards	QS	December 1833	,,	V.D.L.	7 ,,
Ann Jenkin	QS	December 1833	,,	V.D.L.	7 ,,
Mary William	QS	December 1833	,,	V.D.L.	7 ,,
Jane Isaac	QS	April 1834	George Hibbert	N.S.W.	14 ,,
Elizabeth Williams	QS	July 1834	New Grove	V.D.L.	7 ,,
Margaret Williams	QS	October 1834	Mary	N.S.W.	7 ,,
Mary Wallis	QS	January 1835	,,	N.S.W.	7 ,,
Mary Ann Curtis	QS	January 1835	,,	N.S.W.	7 ,,
Hannah Edmunds	Ass.	Feb. 1837	Henry Wellesley	N.S.W.	7 ,,
Elizabeth Anthony	Ass.	March 1838	Planter	N.S.W.	7 ,,
Sarah Powell	QS	October 1838	Hindostan	V.D.L.	15 ,,
Jane Miles	Ass.	February 1841	Garland Grove	V.D.L.	10 ,,
Ann Anthony	QS	October 1840	Emma Eugenia	V.D.L.	7 ,,
Mary Davies	QS	June 1841	,, ,,	V.D.L.	15
Elizabeth Jones	QS	June 1841	,, ,,	V.D.L.	10 ,,
Mary Ann Beddow	QS	April 1840	Royal Admiral	V.D.L.	7 ,,
Margaret Jones	QS	January 1842	,, ,,	V.D.L.	10 ,,
Sarah Davies	Ass.	February 1842	Garland Grove	V.D.L.	10 ,,
Eliza Wheeler	QS	June 1842	,, ,,	V.D.L.	7 ,,
Mary Ann Brewer	QS	October 1844	Tory	V.D.L.	10 ,,
Ann Thomas	QS	June 1845	Emma Eugenia	V.D.L.	7 ,,
Mary Ann Morgan	QS	June 1846	Elizabeth & Henry	V.D.L.	7 ,,
Hannah Williams	QS	June 1847	,,	V.D.L.	10 ,,
Jane Evans	Ass.	July 1847	,,	V.D.L.	7 ,,
Ann Evans	Ass.	July 1847	,,	V.D.L.	—
Margaret Williams	QS	February 1848	Tory	V.D.L.	7 years
Eleanor Watkins	QS	April 1848	Cadet	V.D.L.	7 ,,
Elizabeth Hughes	QS	January 1848	Stately	V.D.L.	7 ,,
Elizabeth Williams	QS	January 1848	,,	V.D.L.	7 ,,
Sarah Morgan	QS	October 1848	,,	V.D.L.	7 ,,
Ann Thomas	QS	October 1848	,,	V.D.L.	7 ,,
Kerziah Jones	QS	July 1849	St. Vincent	V.D.L.	7 ,,
Sarah Davies	Ass.	August 1849	Baretto Junior	V.D.L.	7 ,,

Name	Court	Date of Trial	Ship	Destination	Sentence
Bridget Kelly	QS	January 1850	*Aurora*	V.D.L.	7 ,,
Elizabeth Smith	Ass.	March 1850	,,	V.D.L.	7 ,,
Elizabeth Griffith	Ass.	March 1850	,,	V.D.L.	7 ,,
Catherine Thomas	QS	October 1850	,,	V.D.L.	7 ,,
Maria Meyrick	QS	December 1850	*Anna Maria*	V.D.L.	7 ,,
Mary Ann Powhill	Ass.	February 1851	,, ,,	V.D.L.	7 ,,
Mary Williams	Ass.	February 1851	,, ,,	V.D.L.	7 ,,
Jane Preece	QS	July 1851	,, ,,	V.D.L.	7 ,,
Mary Ann Prosser	QS	July 1851	*Sir Rob. Seppings*	V.D.L.	7 ,,
Sarah Evans	Ass.	March 1852	*Duchess of Northumberland*	V.D.L.	10 ,,
Margaret Jones	QS	June 1852	,,	V.D.L.	7 ,,

Female Transportees—Merionethshire

Name	Court	Date of Trial	Ship	Destination	Sentence
Mary Lewis	GS	April 1793	?	N.S.W.	Life
Eleanor Jones	QS	July 1830	*Earl of Liverpool*	N.S.W.	?
Anne Lewis	QS	July 1833	*Amphitrite*	N.S.W.	7 years
Catherine Pugh	QS	April 1834	*George Hibbert*	N.S.W.	7 ,,
Elizabeth Roberts	QS	October 1837	*Nautilus*	V.D.L.	7 ,,
Ruth Roberts	QS	March 1847	*Cadet*	V.D.L.	7 ,,

Female Transportees—Monmouthshire

Name	Court	Date of Trial	Ship	Destination	Sentence
Eleanor Williams	Ass.	August 1800	*Glatton*	N.S.W.	Life
Mary Thomas	Ass.	March 1801	,,	N.S.W.	7 years
Mary Richards	Ass.	August 1801	,,	N.S.W.	7 ,,
Margaret Phillips	Ass.	August 1801	,,	N.S.W.	7 ,,
Margaret Watkins	Ass.	August 1817	*Maria*	N.S.W.	Life
Mary Morgan	Ass.	August 1824	*Midas*	N.S.W. or V.D.L.	Life
Gwenllian Jones	Ass.	March 1828	*Competitor*	N.S.W.	14 years
Elizabeth Thomas	Ass.	March 1828	,,	N.S.W.	14 ,,
Ann Pike	QS	July 1829	*Eliza*	V.D.L.	14 ,,
Ann Lee	QS	July 1829	,,	V.D.L.	14 ,,
Sarah Waters	Ass.	August 1831	*Pyramus*	N.S.W.	7 ,,
Ann Tippins	Ass.	March 1832	*Fanny*	N.S.W.	14 ,,
Margaret Jones	Ass.	March 1833	*Buffalo*	N.S.W.	7 ,,
Elizabeth Ann Powell	QS	October 1833	*Numa*	N.S.W.	7 ,,
Sarah Ambury	QS	October 1834	*New Grove*	V.D.L.	7 ,,
Ruth Morris	Ass.	November 1835	*Hector*	V.D.L.	14 ,,
Hannah Willis	QS	June 1836	*Westmoreland*	V.D.L.	7 ,,
Amelia Kynvin	Ass.	March 1838	*John Renwick*	N.S.W.	10 ,,

Name	Court	Date of Trial	Ship	Destination	Sentence
Ann Davies	Ass.	March 1838	,, ,,	N.S.W.	7 ,,
Katherine Kelly	Ass.	March 1838	,, ,,	N.S.W.	7 ,,
Charlotte Gilbert	Ass.	July 1838	*Planter*	N.S.W.	15 ,,
Elizabeth Lewis	Ass.	March 1840	*Navarino*	V.D.L.	15 ,,
Ann Watkins	Ass.	March 1840	,,	V.D.L.	10 ,,
Mary Morgan	Ass.	July 1841	*Emma Eugenia*	V.D.L.	7 ,,
Bridget Williams	QS	January 1842	*Royal Admiral*	V.D.L.	10 ,,
Sarah Smart (age 26)	QS	January 1842	,, ,,	V.D.L.	10 ,,
Sarah Smart (age 31)	QS	January 1842	,, ,,	V.D.L.	10 ,,
Mary Williams	Ass.	March 1842	*Garland Grove*	V.D.L.	10 ,,
Charity Hogg	QS	June 1842	,, ,,	V.D.L.	10 ,,
Ann Jones	?	April 1843	*Emma Eugenia*	V.D.L.	7 years
Ann Digget	?	April 1843	,, ,,	V.D.L.	7 ,,
Margaret Coates	Ass.	March 1844	*Tasmania*	V.D.L.	14 ,,
Ann Duffield	Ass.	March 1844	,,	V.D.L.	14 ,,
Mary Cecil	Ass.	March 1844	,,	V.D.L.	10 ,,
Mary Holehouse	QS	October 1844	*Tory*	V.D.L.	7 ,,
Mary Ann Davies	QS	June 1845	*Emma Eugenia*	V.D.L.	14 ,,
Mary Godwin	Ass.	August 1844	*Sea Queen*	V.D.L.	7 ,,
Mary Sullivan	Ass.	April 1846	,, ,,	V.D.L.	10 ,,
Elizabeth Jones	QS	January 1847	*Cadet*	V.D.L.	7 ,,
Ann Griffiths	Ass.	April 1847	,,	V.D.L.	10 ,,
Catherine Butcher	Ass.	April 1847	,,	V.D.L.	7 ,,
Caroline Jones	QS	June 1847	*Elizabeth & Henry*	V.D.L.	7 ,,
Margaret Payne	QS	June 1847	*Tory*	V.D.L.	7 ,,
Phoebe Hodge	QS	October 1847	,,	V.D.L.	10 ,,
Mary Jenkins	QS	October 1848	*Stateley*	V.D.L.	10 ,,
Mary Jones	QS	October 1848	,,	V.D.L.	10 ,,
Margaret Phillips	QS	October 1848	,,	V.D.L.	10 ,,
Jane Watson	QS	October 1848	,,	V.D.L.	10 ,,
Emma Rowles	Ass.	August 1849	*Baretto Junior*	V.D.L.	10 ,,
Ann Rees	QS	October 1849	,, ,,	V.D.L.	7 ,,
Eliza Tipper	QS	December 1849	*Emma Eugenia*	V.D.L.	7 ,,
Eliza Bevan	Ass.	August 1850	*Aurora*	V.D.L.	15 ,,
Catherine Preece	Ass.	August 1850	,,	V.D.L.	15 ,,
Mary Jane Stephen	Ass.	August 1850	,,	V.D.L.	10 ,,
Margaret Coghlan	QS	December 1850	,,	V.D.L.	7 ,,
Ellen Jones	QS	June 1851	*Anna Maria*	V.D.L.	10 ,,
Margaret Williams	Ass.	August 1851	*Duchess of Northumberland*	V.D.L.	7 ,,
Elizabeth Warren	QS	February 1852	,,	V.D.L.	10 ,,
Eliza Dove	Ass.	March 1852	,,	V.D.L.	Life
Harriet Symonds (al. Martha Davies)	QS	June 1852	,,	V.D.L.	10 years

Female Transportees—Montgomeryshire

Name	Court	Date of Trial	Ship	Destination	Sentence
Ann Glossop	GS	March 1791	The Pitt	N.S.W.	7 years
Margaret Richards/ Somer	GS	August 1801	Glatton	N.S.W.	14 ''
Mary Griffiths	GS	August 1801	''	N.S.W.	7 ''
Jane Owen	GS	March 1804	William Pitt	N.S.W.	7 ''
Ann Evans (al. Nancy Walters)	GS (?)	January 1810	Admiral Gambier	N.S.W.	7 ''
Maria Jones	GS	April 1818	Lord Wellington	N.S.W.	Life
Mary Hughes	GS	March 1818	Janus	N.S.W.	7 years
Mary Blakenore	QS	July 1818	''	N.S.W.	7 ''
Hannah Fox (al. wife of J. Ponty)	QS	July 1827	Louisa	N.S.W.	7 ''
Elizabeth Williams	GS	March 1827	Borneo	V.D.L.	Life
Louisa Roberts	GS	August 1829	Eliza	V.D.L.	7 years
Elizabeth Jones		October 1833	Numa	N.S.W.	7 ''
Sarah Gane		October 1833	''	N.S.W.	7 ''
Ann Roberts	QS	July 1834	Arab	V.D.L.	7 ''
Ann Bennett	QS	January 1836	Elizabeth	N.S.W.	14 ''
Mary Ann Aubrey	QS	January 1839	Hindostan	V.D.L.	10 ''
Rosetta Oliver	QS	January 1843	Emma Eugenia	V.D.L.	7 ''
Margaret Insell	QS	February 1844	Tasmania	V.D.L.	7 ''
Mary Rogers	QS	January 1846	Sea Queen	V.D.L.	7 ''
Eliza Thomas	QS	January 1847	Cadet	V.D.L.	10 ''
Fanny Bennett	QS	October 1848	Stateley	V.D.L.	7 ''
Elizabeth Davies (al. Grist)	QS	January 1849	St. Vincent	V.D.L.	7 ''

Female Transportees—Pembrokeshire

Name	Court	Date of Trial	Ship	Destination	Sentence
Martha Morgan	QS	October 1786	Neptune	N.S.W.	7 years
Jane Codd	QS	January 1788	Atlantic	N.S.W.	7 ''
Catherine Owen	GS	August 1800	Experiment	N.S.W.	7 ''
Mary Lawrence	GS	April 1801	''	N.S.W.	7 ''
Mary Davies	QS	July 1801	''	N.S.W.	7 ''
Sophia Jones	GS	August 1801	''	N.S.W.	Life
Mary Davies	GS	August 1826	Harmony	N.S.W.	7 years
Ann Morgan	QS	October 1827	Borneo	V.D.L.	7 ''
Ann, wife of Philip Gwyn	GS	April 1830	Kains	N.S.W.	Life
Ann Gwyther	Ass.	July 1833	Numa	N.S.W.	10 years
Mary Hay	Ass.	March 1837	Henry Wellesley	N.S.W.	14 ''
Sarah Rees	QS	October 1837	Nautilus	V.D.L.	7 ''
Mary Burns	QS	January 1839	Hindostan	V.D.L.	7 ''
Ann Roberts	QS	July 1840	Navarino	V.D.L.	7 ''

Name	Court	Date of Trial	Ship	Destination	Sentence
Anne Jenkins	QS	October 1841	*Royal Admiral*	V.D.L.	10 ʼʼ
Hannah Oliver	Ass.	March 1851	*Anna Maria*	V.D.L.	7 ʼʼ
Hannah John	Ass.	July 1850	*Sir Robert Seppings*	V.D.L.	7 ʼʼ

Female Transportees—Radnorshire

Name	Court	Date of Trial	Ship	Destination	Sentence
Margaret Clarke	GS	April 1788	*Neptune*	N.S.W.	7 years
Sarah Chandler	GS	April 1817	*Friendship*	N.S.W.	Life
Ann Morgan	QS	April 1828	*Princess Royal*	N.S.W.	7 years
Ann Syar	?	August 1831	*Burrell*	N.S.W.	Life
Margaret Saunders	QS	January 1833	*Buffalo*	N.S.W.	7 years
Ann Jones	Ass.	August 1835	*Arab*	V.D.L.	Life
Mary Jones	Ass.	August 1835	ʼʼ	V.D.L.	14 years
Mary Probart (al. Davies)	QS	October 1845	*Sea Queen*	V.D.L.	10 ʼʼ
Elizabeth Morris	QS	January 1846	ʼʼ ʼʼ	V.D.L.	7 ʼʼ

SHORT BIBLIOGRAPHY

Contemporary Works

Books

M. Carpenter	—	*Reformatory Schools for the Children of the Perishing and Dangerous Classes*	(1851)
G. L. Chesterton	—	*Revelations of Prison Life*	(1856)
A. Griffiths	—	*Memorials of Millbank*	(1884)
W. Hoyle	—	*Crime in England and Wales in the Nineteenth Century*	(1876)
C. Lombroso	—	*The Female Offender* (English Translation, New York 1898)	
	—	*Memoir of and Life of Elizabeth Fry edited by her two daughters*	(1847)
F. W. Robinson	—	*Female Life in Prison by a Prison Matron*	(1862)
H. Richards	—	*Letters on the Social and Political Conditions of Wales*	(1866)
J. C. Symons	—	*Tactics for the Times as regards the Condition and Treatment of the Dangerous Classes*	(1849)
T. Timpson	—	*Memoirs of Elizabeth Fry*	(1847)

Articles

Anonymous	—	'Criminal Women', *Cornhill Magazine*, XIV Aug. pp. 152-160	(1866)

Modern

C. Bateson	—	*The Convict Ships*	(1959)
M. Dixson	—	*The Real Mathilda: Women and Identity in Australia 1788 to 1975*	(1976)
L. L. Robson		*The Convict Settlers of Australia*	(1970)
A. G. L. Shaw	—	*Convicts and the Colonies*	(1966)
A. Smith	—	*Women in Prison*	(1962)
A. Summers	—	*Damned Whores and God's Police*	(1975)
J. J. Tobias	—	*Crime and Industrial Society in the Nineteenth Century*	(1967)

165

Articles

R. C. Hutchinson — 'Mrs. Hutchinson and the Female Factories of Early Australia', Tasmanian Historical Research Association, *Papers and Proceedings*, Vol. II No. 2 Dec. 1963

H. S. Payne — 'A Statistical Study of Female Convicts in Tasmania 1843-1853'. *Ibid.* Vol. 9 No. 2 June 1961

D. Beddoe — 'Carmarthenshire Women and Criminal Transportation to Australia', *The Carmarthenshire Antiquary* 1978

,,   ,, — 'Eleanor James: Cardigan's only Female Transportee', *Ceredigion*, 1979